HOW TO BE OUTRAGEOUSLY SUCCESSFUL WITH WOMEN

HOW TO BE OUTRAGEOUSLY SUCCESSFUL WITH WOMEN

by John Mack Carter & Lois Wyse

William Morrow and Company, Inc.

New York

1975

Printed in the United States of America.
    2   3   4   5   79   78   77   76   75

Book design by Lubalin, Smith, Carnase, Inc.

Library of Congress Cataloging in Publication Data
Carter, John Mack.
    How to be outrageously successful with women.
    1. Women—Psychology. 2. Sex role. 3. Etiquette—United
States. 4. Interpersonal relations. I. Wyse, Lois, joint au-
thor. II. Title.
HQ1206.C27   395′.1′232   75-15789
ISBN 0-688-02940-X

INTRODUCTION

The idea for writing a guidebook to the sexual revolution came to John Mack Carter one day as he was on his way from *McCall's* to *Ladies' Home Journal.* During the twenty years he has been editing magazines for women, the only thing that has changed more than the magazine business (whatever happened to *The Saturday Evening Post, Collier's, Liberty, Woman's Home Companion?*) is women (whatever became of women who were seen but not heard, volunteer workers, and garden clubs?).

John called Lois Wyse, an advertising executive who is a sometime writer and a full-time woman, and asked her what she thought of the idea of co-authoring a book about women, a book addressed to men. Lois immediately put a new ribbon in her typewriter, because she agreed that most male chauvinists and female detractors needed instructions in order to deal with the new kind of woman who is infiltrating business, the professions, and even the home.

The authors believe that women, as well as men, have been affected by the changes that began in the 1960s. The new woman is turning out to be a humanity-oriented person who seeks to create a better world for herself and for others. She does not necessarily hold a job or command headlines when she speaks, but she is more visible, more powerful—and maybe more uncertain than ever. For these reasons men must relearn what they once knew about women. The old rules don't apply; the old myths are dying. Even though woman's view of herself and man's view of her role have changed considerably, not everything has changed. Good manners are still good manners. Holding a door and extending a helping hand are still offers a woman can accept without compromising her belief in equal opportunities.

As women seek more chances to be vocal about their own destinies, as they reach toward such traditional male power strongholds as mayors' offices and corporate boardrooms, one cannot lose sight of the fact that women are not the same as men.

Men and women have been conditioned to be different from one another, and it is that difference we must reckon with. All of us have to understand that women still want to be women and not ersatz men. All of us have to understand that men have adjustments to make, too, and not all of them are simple.

Despite the raising of consciousness concerning women and their roles, there is still a tremendous amount of guilt, anxiety, and uncertainty men share with men and women share with women.

The man-woman relationship and the woman-woman relationship are both changing all the time, for they are built on needs that vary according to the situation. This book is about many situations and the ways to resolve them so that both you and the woman find satisfaction.

Anybody can live. John Mack Carter and Lois Wyse want you to live better.

It isn't easy.

You have to give before you can take.

You have to open your head and your heart, clean out the cobwebs, and treat a woman right. As right as you'd treat a man.

That isn't always easy. Or possible.

But here's how to try. This book should work, providing you use it. Like the Pill, it doesn't help just to have it in the drawer.

ADVENTURES

Go ahead and have one. At least one.

Once in your life do what you want to do.

Stop worrying about what everyone will say. Chances are "everyone" doesn't give a damn. Most lives are a diet of drabness relieved by an occasional good time, darkened by an occasional tragedy.

If the chance to live comes along, take it.

Once there was a man who hailed a cab in Chicago's Loop only to find that the driver stopped a few feet behind him to pick up a beautiful young woman. She put her hand on the cab door, turned to the man at the curb, and said, "Want to share the cab?"

"I'm going north," he said.

She shrugged. "Wrong direction." Then she stepped into the cab and drove away. Seconds later the cab screeched to a halt, and the young woman put her head out the window. "You'll always wonder what would have happened if you had shared this cab," she said.

She was right. He has never stopped wondering.

ADVERSARIES, ENEMIES, AND THE LOYAL OPPOSITION

No role becomes a woman less—or is thrust on her more often—than the adversary position. Generally it is men who finger the women who will serve as their conscience, their moderator, their stand-in mother, and then they direct their anger and hostility against these women in the guise of something fine and good.

So, if in the name of friendship you find yourself doing any of these things . . . stop!

1. If you use your wife as the live-in reason for your good behavior, stop. She is not a truant officer. Either admit *you* don't want to hurt your relationship or act the way you want to.

2. If you fail to give your wife moral and vocal support in disagreements with family, friends, or co-workers, stop. Start putting your actions where you claim your feelings are . . . or else sort out your feelings and find why you are inwardly glad when someone else is outwardly hostile to your wife.

3. If you blame your secretary every time you forget to attend a meeting, write a memo, or phone home, stop. Your secretary does not want to sound like a dummy any more than you do.

ADVERSITY

You do not need to read the front page of the newspaper to know that economic conditions are not what they used to be. The go-go days of the sixties are behind us, and most of us are victims of some kind of economic frustration.

How people handle adversity is as much a test of their character as the way they handle success. Job losses, cuts in salary, or reduced working hours should be faced squarely with the woman in your life.

Some men still believe that the best way to handle bad days is to pretend they did not happen. Maybe that works with Barbie dolls and other equally animate sex symbols, but a real live woman can face tough times if she is told the truth. She'll find it easier to economize if you let her know the reasons for doing so. Some people even find that the man-woman relationship becomes closer and more necessary in troubled days.

ADVICE

man gets his investment advice from his barber and his restaurant tips from cab drivers. But when does he seek out his female friend for advice? Usually it is exclusively in matters of romance, and generally it concerns a wife he wants to shed. He thinks he knows what his female friend will advise and asks only to hear the answer he wants.

The man who asks his wife for advice on business is still on the drawing board. Yet there is nobody but nobody better equipped to give you the right answer to any business problem you have—whether it's magazines or munitions—than your wife.

You forget how much she knows about your business just by listening to your boasting and complaining for years. And she may know you better than you know yourself.

Peter Drucker pales by comparison, because he doesn't know your business or your quirks.

AGE

Take a thirty-five-year-old woman and treat her like a seven-year-old . . . and what do you have?

An annoyed thirty-five-year-old woman.

Questions never to ask a grown woman (or a small child) include:

- Is this your first job?
  (If she has an important job, that's not just a put-down of women; it is a corporate insult.)
- Are you old enough to drink?
  (Oh, come on, you didn't really mean that . . . so why say it?)
- How old are you?
  (If she does her job well, what's the difference?)
- How did a kid like you get a job like this?
  (If you accompany the question with a king-sized leer, you can be sure she'll never tell.)

AGGRESSIVENESS

oo much aggressiveness on her part gives men and women more problems than too little sex. The word "aggressive" is one of those sexual words; it means something good when applied to men and something negative when applied to women. This is not so much because of aggressiveness itself as it is the way aggressiveness is perceived by men. Men see the aggressive woman as one who asserts herself at the expense of others, one who seeks to dominate, and one who may be hostile.

In order to cope with female aggressiveness (some of which indeed may be based on assertion, dominance, and hostility) men have to be strong themselves. You have to be an independent thinker able to judge the aggressive woman on the basis of her talents and ideas rather than judge the motivation for her aggressiveness.

Or next thing you know she might be judging the motivation for yours.

AGING

Someone once said that age is a state of mind. Unfortunately the truth of that aphorism does not make aging any easier to deal with. In understanding a woman, it is important to remember that her psychological age may not always match your idea of her numerical age.

At twenty-five she needs help in understanding she cannot be a child any longer. It is very hard to put away the toys of childhood in order to accept a world made ugly by grown-ups.

At thirty she has taken a giant step into adulthood, but she still feels twenty-five.

And so it goes, each five-year period another milestone, another signpost toward . . . what?

What a woman needs most in order to accept her inevitable aging is less emphasis on a youthful appearance by society in general and more respect for accomplishment than appearance.

Men, of course, need the very same thing. A toupee never covered a bald spot in the intelligence.

Matching and mating while growing older is hard for a man and even more difficult for a woman because society accepts the older

man/younger woman pairing with more grace
than it does the younger man/older woman.
Prospects for marriage or relationships diminish
with a woman's age. An eighty-year-old woman
once put it this way: "I would get married again,
but sixty isn't interested; seventy is married;
eighty is sick; and ninety is dead."

AMATEUR PSYCHIATRY

If you don't have
the training, don't play the role of pro. For every
woman with a problem, there is a man who can
analyze it with pop-psych words like
ambivalence, duality, inner strength, and
outer-directed.

Giving advice is like playing with matches.
Before you settle down to the long-term role of
counselor, be certain the advice you give is
advice she can live with.

Besides, most women do not really want
advice. What they seek is sympathy and
understanding—and you don't have to be a
psychiatrist to give lots of that.

APPROACHES

It comes as a shock to most men, but women are approachable. They are as lonely and bored as men, as eager to change their lives, and as willing to gamble on the consequences.

There are some points to remember in approaching a woman, however:

1. If you want a lasting relationship, don't look for the woman who is the belle of the bar.
2. Don't be afraid to approach a beautiful woman; she wants love and warmth just as much as the less attractive one you think will accept you. And who knows? That beautiful woman may be able to see beyond your crooked nose into your superior character, intellect, and personality.
3. Learn to talk to a woman the way you talk to a man: with humor, tolerance, interest.
4. If you don't seem to hit it off well the first time around and her credentials are good, try again. Maybe the chemistry was wrong the first time. First-rate people deserve a second chance.

ARGUMENTS

here is a story about a couple married for thirty-three years who never had a cross word or an argument. Then, the thirty-fourth year, they were divorced.

Arguing is as much a part of a relationship as agreeing. It is the style and spirit with which discussions are held that result in couples coming closer or drifting further apart when they disagree.

When arguing with any woman—your mother, wife, sister, daughter, employer, or employee—don't use sexism in your rejoinders. Don't tell her she is emotional (just like a woman), irrational (just like a woman), illogical, nagging, etc., ad inf. Such tactics amount to name calling and not only weaken your offense or defense, they weaken your relationship.

So fight when you must, but fight fair.

AUTHORITY (ACCEPTING WOMEN IN)

Ever since women started to do something besides teach school, give piano lessons, and dust some male boss's desk, the business world has been getting used to female decisions. Yet it is difficult for some men to accept a woman who is empowered to say more than "no." It is difficult for some men to realize that women have not only authority but also their own way of doing things.

Two months after a woman product manager of a major pharmaceutical company succeeded her male boss, subordinates still said, "Jim wouldn't have done it that way," or "Jim doesn't like that."

The woman executive does not think the toughest thing about her job is the increased responsibility, worry over budgets, and concern with manufacturing problems. Her biggest obstacle is getting people to understand that it doesn't matter what Jim would do.

BATHING, SCENTS, AND SUCH

Of course it is ridiculous to include something so mundane as washing behind the ears in a book filled with lofty ideals, intellectual byplay, and commonsense business practice. But still the fact remains that a man does not score points on bad breath or bad anything else.

Since you expect her to do little things like bathe before lovemaking, add a few scents where it counts, doesn't it make sense for you to do the same? Well, at least before you knock it, try it.

BEDTIME

If there is one time to forget what *they* want and concentrate solely on what *she*—and *you*—want, it is bedtime.

In case you have not heard, what happens in bed must please not only you, but her, too. And here are some of the things that should bring pleasure to you both:

1. A realization that sexual activity is personal; nobody is grading you two. If it pleases you and her, it must be good.
2. There is no one way for a woman to look in bed. If you want her in a black diaphanous gown and she wears one, great. If she loves her shortie pajama tops, let her wear them. What's the difference?
3. It does not matter who instigates the lovemaking; women have needs, too, and a man should be flattered, not flustered, when the woman is the aggressor.
4. Equality in and out of bed does not have to mean the end of romance. For instance, women can still be perfumed

and powdered if you both like that. The real equality in the bedroom comes in mutual awareness of needs and responsibility to fill those needs.

BEING
INTERVIEWED BY

The fact that you've never worked for a woman doesn't mean you don't want this job.

When you're sitting in your prospective female boss's office, remember that you have all the usual opportunities for mistakes plus a host of new ones. Here are some ways to move from candidate to officeholder:

First, listen carefully to the introduction the secretary makes. Just because the woman in the corner office is married doesn't mean that she wants to be called Mrs. Listen for the Miss or Mrs., and if it comes out Ms., use it.

Second, wait to be invited to sit down. And wait for an indication that smoking is okay. If in doubt, don't smoke.

When you meet her, you will be aware of the three of you: she, you, and it. "It" is the idea of a woman boss. It will not come between you unless you invite it. When you open your mouth, say something to advance your cause. Don't mouth simple nothings. She knows her office is well decorated, that the anemones are pretty, that her dress is becoming. Tell her what she doesn't know: what you can do for her company, not for her.

She doesn't want to hear that you've never worked for a woman before. She can tell that.

She too is wondering how well you can work for a woman, but she won't be bashful about asking if she wants to hear your answer. The only answer that makes any sense is that it won't make any difference.

And it won't, if you do your job.

Oh yes, try for once to look her in the eye. You aren't there to appraise her legs.

BELLHOPS, HAT CHECKERS, CAR PARKERS

Okay. So there she is with a fistful of cash and a super expense account. You go out for lunch, and she signs the bill. Neat. Now you approach the checkroom, where her briefcase, your coat, and one umbrella are waiting to be picked up. The hat checker smiles. So do you. So does the woman you're with. Now, who reaches for the quarter tip?

You do.

Because the woman you are with may be free as a bird, wild as the wind, rich as a rock star . . . but you can be sure she is not so liberated that she wants to tip a hat checker, bellhop, or parking lot attendant.

It's your turn to pay this one.

BIRTH CONTROL

Boys used to sneak into drugstores, buy a package of condoms, and then hope to get a chance to use them. With the advent of the Pill and the Loop, however, sex etiquette has come a long, long way.

If you are going to bed with a woman for the first time, find out what she is doing about birth control. Is the question too personal? Well, you were just about to get into bed with her, weren't you?

If she is your regular girl friend, no reason you

should not share the cost of the Pill that she takes. Similarly you can share or pay for her gynecological visits to get and fit an IUD. And she must be equally supportive if you decide on a vasectomy.

Sex is no longer simply something she gives and you take. It is—finally—a totally shared experience.

BLIND DATES

 lot has changed between men and women, but the blind date goes on and on. You know all the little tricks, of course. Call a strange woman for a drink, and if she gets past the first ice cube, take her to dinner. Of course, you never commit yourself to a long evening or an event with people you care about if you are taking a woman you have never met. Blind dates are usually misplaced hope, but occasionally they work out.

One editor tells about the widowed surgeon who came to take her to dinner.

"It was a routine for him. You knew that he had absolutely no regard for women," she said. "It was all a ritual. I went to the door, and he thrust one of those end-of-the-day, twenty-five-cents-a-bunch wilted roses at me. Instead of a necktie he wore a leather cord with a silver slide. His dyed hair was combed in bangs over his forehead and flipped up to hide his receding hairline. He had on an electric blue double-knit suit. And that was only the beginning.

"We went to a restaurant for dinner, and during dinner he never once asked about me. He never asked what I did, what my opinions were about anything in the world. I was just there, this object put there to listen to him talk.

"During dinner I felt him grab the inside of my thigh. I thought I would die. 'What are you doing?' I asked. 'I'm just checking to see why you think you're too fat.' I am exactly three pounds overweight, and I didn't need him to check me out.

"I couldn't end the evening fast enough. But it was obviously his idea that if a woman accepted a blind date, she was simply a sex object. You handed her the perfunctory floral offering, fed her, and then jumped her. Didn't he know the only reason I went was that my mother would have been upset if I refused a date with a doctor, especially a surgeon?"

Blind dates, in short, are like all other dates. They are to be treated like new acquaintances, not second-class citizens. And they are never, never to be considered objects . . . as opposed to the real people you pick for yourself.

THE
BOARD MEMBER
(PART I)

Corporate America discovered blacks and women almost simultaneously, and in the rush to be the first on the block with a minority board member, major corporations found themselves wooing the same people at the same time. It was almost as if there weren't enough minority representatives to fill the boardrooms of America.

In fact, big business had such a hard time finding people they kept appointing the same ones again and again. For instance, **Catherine B. Clary,** the potent president of Milwaukee's First Wisconsin Trust Co., an old-timer on major boards (she has been on General Motors' Board since 1972), is also a director of AT&T, Kraftco, and Northwestern Mutual Life Insurance. **Patricia Roberts Harris,** the Washington attorney, who is not only a woman but is also black and so fits two categories, sits on the boards of IBM, Chase Manhattan Bank, and Scott Paper Co.

With so much duplication it appears obvious that executives cull the same lists of candidates.

So, as a public service to major corporations, here are a few new names:

Gloria Steinem   Not new, you say? Yes, she
    would be a new face in corporate
    boardrooms because, despite her obvious
    intelligence and ability to communicate,
    she is not (as of this writing) on the board
    of a single corporation!
Billie Jean King   She could fire a few strong
    ideas in the boardroom of a sports
    team—or a major corporation.

And there are many others who have major contributions to make:

Anne Armstrong   Member, Cost of Living
    Council; former counselor to President
    Nixon
Shirley Temple Black   Ambassador to Ghana;
    former Representative to the General
    Assembly of the United Nations
Dr. Mary S. Calderone   Executive Director, Sex
    Information and Education Council of the
    United States (SIECUS); editor, *Manual of
    Family Planning and Contraceptive Practice*
Elizabeth Carpenter   Vice-president, Hill &
    Knowlton, Inc., Public Relations; former
    press secretary and staff director to Mrs.
    Lyndon B. Johnson
Helen K. Copley   Chief executive, Copley
    Newspaper Corporation
Charlotte Curtis   Associate Editor, *The New
    York Times;* member, Manhattan advisory
    board of New York Urban League
Renee DuJean   Director, National Urban
    League's Black Executive Exchange
    Program

Myrlie Evers   Contributing editor, *Ladies' Home Journal;* former Democratic Congressional candidate, California, 1970

Sissy Farenthold   Political activist and practicing lawyer; former member, Texas House of Representatives, 1968–1972; Democratic candidate for Governor of Texas, 1972

Mary Joan Glynn   President, Simplicity Pattern Company

Martha W. Griffiths   Former Democratic representative from Michigan, 84th to 92nd Congresses

Elinor Guggenheimer   Consumer Affairs Commissioner, City of New York

Dr. Matina Horner   President and Dean, Radcliffe College

Elizabeth Janeway   Trustee, Barnard College; author, *Man's World, Woman's Place* and *Between Myth and Morning*

Mary Conway Kohler   Director, National Commission on Resources for Youth, Inc.

Juanita M. Kreps   Professor of Economics and vice-president, Duke University; member, Board of Directors of National Council on Aging

Alice Tepper Marlin   Founder and Executive Director, Council on Economic Priorities

Mary Adelaide Mendelson   Housewife who broke the nursing home scandal with her book *Tender Loving Greed;* member, Governor's Task Force on Nursing Homes (Ohio)

Betty Southard Murphy   Member, NLRB

Esther Peterson   Consumer adviser, Giant Food Company; former special assistant to President Lyndon B. Johnson for consumer affairs

Marlene Sanders Producer, ABC Television
News Documentary Unit
Eleanor Bernert Sheldon President, Social
Science Research Council
Marciarose Shistack Newspaperwoman and
television personality
Barbara Sizemore Superintendent of public
schools, Washington, D.C.
Barbara Doran Sullivan National director of
Consumer Affairs, The Great Atlantic &
Pacific Tea Company (A&P Food Stores)
Judith Thayer Partner, New York law firm of
Paul, Weiss, Rifkind, Wharton & Garrison
Margaret Bush Wilson Chairman, NAACP
Dr. Nina Woodside Director, Center for
Women in Medicine, Medical College of
Pennsylvania; member and secretary,
HEW's Advisory Council on Rights &
Responsibilities of Women

THE BOARD MEMBER (PART II)

Despite the fact that more women are being appointed to boards, their membership frequently represents tokenism. Most women are appointed for the public relations value and not for the contributions they can make. Like the token Catholic, the token Jew, and the token black, the token woman is there to approve policies, not to upset the corporation.

The best way a woman can contribute is to have a specific assignment commensurate with her talents and capabilities. If that is done, it doesn't matter whether she is a woman or not. That, of course, is the way all boards should function. Tokenism—racial, religious, professional, or sexist—is as meaningless at the board level as it is within the ranks.

BRAGGING, BOASTING, AND SELF-EXPLOITATION

Some men cannot help it. It just comes on them like tennis elbow or indigestion. They have to tell the world they have the car with the most mileage and the secretary with the least. They have to impress a woman. The man who has seen, done, tried everything—and announces it as regularly as a station break—succeeds everywhere but with women.

Of course women admire power and success, but not when the success object points it out. What you do is always more impressive than what you say you do.

BRAINS

I f you have any, give the other sex equal credit and end the argument before you lose it.

His and Her brains are the same size, but they do work differently. That doesn't mean that different is better; different means most of us have been conditioned by different training and experiences.

Women do think differently from men, and when a man and woman think together, they can lick any man in the house.

THE BRIDE

If she married you less than a year ago, you're right. She is your bride. Anything more, and she's your wife. The gray-haired man who peers over his potbelly to introduce "my bride" is not enhancing her role. He is demeaning it.

Women have a right to be known as "my wife," and men have no right to treat them like dutifully decorative objects with an insipid introduction like "my bride."

Incidentally, that also holds true for men who speak of "the old lady," * "the little woman," and "my better half." They are all clichés for what these husbands obviously regard as the all-time cliché of their lives: marriage.

---

* Not to be confused with "my old lady," a reference made by unmarried men to the women who live with them.

CASTRATING WOMEN AND OTHER CONTEMPORARY BITCHES

There is a lot that is new about women. But some things are not. There are still castrating women and bitches.

Castrating women are not easily recognizable. Some people believe that a woman with power is automatically a castrating woman. False. A woman with power is nothing but a woman with power.

However, a woman with power is castrating when she fails to hire strong men and women to work under her, but delights instead in hiring people with heavy problems such as drug addiction, alcoholism, or wife-beating. A castrating woman then uses these problems to keep her employees locked in place through a combination of fear and gratitude.

Castrating women have long operated on husbands and sons. Now they are at work in work. But only in middle and upper management.

Bitches, both male and female, are at every level of business. And you don't need a book to recognize one.

CHANGES

In every dealing with women, it pays to remember—every woman's life has changed. If most of what you know about women came from your mother, go to the foot of the class and contemplate the effect of these major changes in women's lives today:

1. Increased education. Higher education for women no longer means Katharine Gibbs.
2. Increased employment outside the home. Almost every woman can, and half of them do. Just think about how *you've* changed in the years between asking for a weekly allowance and earning a paycheck.
3. Changing role within the family. Your wife and the Census Bureau may give you credit for being the head of the household, but don't ask anybody else about who runs the house unless you can stand the truth. No longer does the Home Guard line up respectfully and salute when the king comes home each evening. Or hadn't you noticed?

4. The economy. Affluence, inflation, and recession. Handling money ages a body. Balancing a budget in times of galloping prices produces instant maturity.

CHANGES IN THINKING

It may be only a popular illusion that the whole world has turned upside down. However, in the case of women, it has. These are the principal symptoms:

1. Decline of old authorities. Nothing personal here, because you haven't been regarded as an authority for some time now. The victims of this decline are such institutions as the government (a casualty of the Vietnam War and Watergate) and the church (a casualty of birth control, abortion, and divorce).
2. Changes in the value system. It used to be that everything was okay if a woman

kept a spotless house, worked hard, and imbibed only on Saturday night. As the song asks, "Is this all there is?" Not today.

3. Emphasis on the youth market. Mass marketers have convinced us that being young isn't everything, it's the only thing. If we can't be young, then we must look young and act young and pretend young.

4. Consumers. When the first Denver housewife took up her post in front of the supermarket to start the boycott against beef, the whole world tilted just a bit. Since then, all of us have begun to understand that the voice of the individual consumer can ring in the ears of government and business, and a new feeling is abroad in the land. It's called consumer power.

5. Women's liberation. Betty Friedan dropped a pebble in the ocean. It was a book called *The Feminine Mystique*. It was ridiculed, revered, imitated, and now cannot be ignored.

CHARGE!

In the Cinderella legend she is poor, he is rich, and so there is no question whose American Express card is used.

Nowadays there's a good chance that she has more money than he—so who pays for what? She's still operating under the old rules that say if he loves her, he pays for her. And even if he doesn't love her, he still feeds her.

Here are the new rules about money:

1. Go Dutch whenever you can afford it. If you always split expenses, you can stay cool about cash and save your emotions for the good stuff.
2. If you're a man who finds she picks up most of the checks, learn to give her a lot of presents—wildflowers, leaves, poems you copy in your own handwriting. In other words, let her know she is getting her money's worth.
3. Don't think you owe her too much because she pays.
4. Don't take advantage of a woman with money. She'd rather be loved for a lot of other reasons.

CHEEK

lice Duer Miller, the American novelist and poet, wrote in 1915:

WHY WE
OPPOSE VOTES
FOR MEN

1. Because man's place is in the army.
2. Because no really manly man wants to settle any question otherwise than by fighting about it.
3. Because if men should adopt peaceable methods women will no longer look up to them.
4. Because men will lose their charm if they step out of their natural sphere and interest themselves in other matters than feats of arms, uniforms and drums.
5. Because men are too emotional to vote. Their conduct at baseball games and political conventions shows this, while their innate tendency to appeal to force renders them particularly unfit for the task of government.

CIGARS

It has long been held that women don't like the smell of cigars, that cigar smoke clings to clothes and hair, that cigar smoking is an especially obnoxious habit.

It's all true.

It isn't enough to pull out a big black cigar after dinner, clip the end, moisten the bit all around, toast the edge over a flame, then look at the hostess with concern and ask, "Will this bother you?" Of course it will bother her, unless she intends to spend the rest of the evening out in the parking lot.

The woman who insists she loves the smell of cigar smoke because it reminds her of her father, who remarks that it is such a manly habit, who insists on serving as your first assistant during the prolonged ritual, probably is breathing through her mouth and lying through her teeth.

Don't smoke them in the office meeting. Don't smoke them at the table. Don't smoke them in the car.

. Try the closet.

CLEANLINESS IS NEXT TO MANLINESS

It is obviously a machine designed for use by a man. It is heavy to pull around. It is complicated. Every thrust takes the equivalent of a strong golf swing.

"It" is the vacuum cleaner.

If your mate now manages all the cleaning work herself, make a deal with her. At least one week a month take over all the vacuuming chores.

Ask her to make out a schedule of the rooms to be vacuumed. Then see if you can stick to it.

Just think how much fun it will be when you ask her to lift her feet.

COCKTAIL PARTY CONVERSATION WITH A WOMAN WHO WORKS

Men like to talk to men about the market, golf scores, and women. They also like to talk to women. But men do not know what to say. If the woman stays at home, he will indulgently ask about her children and turn off if she tells him. Or he will ask about her political or PTA activity, and when she indicates she is both serious and committed, he turns off. Or he will talk about her body—and then wonder why she turns off.

Most men have never really learned to talk to women who have little in common with them (or so they think). And now that women are working in far greater numbers than ever before, men are even more baffled about what to say to women who may know more than they do.

Probably 90 percent of all men are uncomfortable with a woman who works. But if men would just unbend and talk to women like people, they would have a lot less difficulty. Most women aren't attracted to men because men are so handsome. (Is Kissinger gorgeous?) Power men have a sex appeal pretty boys never achieve. The same is true of women. Smart, aware women can arouse men to new, higher levels of understanding. But men have to open themselves for the experience. They can't be defensive or make deprecating remarks.

Conversation is like sex. The more you think of her, the better it gets for you.

COMMERCIALS

She stands in front of a refrigerator, next to a washing machine, or clutches an aspirin bottle. She is Woman, long-suffering and in need of help, help that seems to come only from detergent breakthroughs or pain relievers. Or so you would believe if all your opinions of women were based on the women you see in commercials.

Most of us know that these exaggerated life situations are not typical of women, but this kind of negative advertising indirectly influences all our thinking about men and women.

For instance . . .

Do you think women have more headaches than men? (A recent study shows that doctors believe they do, and the reason they believe it is that women, more than men, star in pain commercials. As a result of this study you will soon be seeing more men holding their heads in their hands on TV.)

Do you think it unmanly to dust? (Women on TV are the ones who find all the new furniture polishes and learn to love them more than their husbands, children, and the old furniture polish.)

When you find sexism in commercials, don't just stew. Write a letter. Sometimes advertisers and their agencies unwittingly produce sexist commercials.

Lois Wyse once wrote a radio commercial for Smucker's that said, "Everybody knows women are better cooks than men." An astute Californian wrote a complaining letter to Smucker's, and the spot was immediately taken off the air and rewritten.

Advertisers do listen to intelligent, forthright complaints about their advertising, so there is something you can do besides turn off the radio or TV set.

COMPARISONS

It is not really a male thing; it is a people thing—that tendency to make comparisons. Is she as pretty as the one in the corner? Who's smarter, you or I?

Liberated men, like all men, will continue to make comparisons, but comparisons must be made with new and different values. Men will find that awareness of women as people and not objects tends to increase their sensitivity toward all persons.

Judgments can be made on the basis of significant values, and to do that men need to remind themselves that they do not enhance their own stature when they judge or compare on the basis of size of breasts, seductive walk, or turn of calf.

COMPETITION

If you really have competitive spirit, it is not the men and women with whom you work that you compete with. Your real competitor is you. Instead of wasting energy wondering what he or she will do or what someone else's reaction will be, you continually try to do yourself one better.

You look for challenges that give you more than financial reward. You try to do things that are socially worthwhile and make life better for someone else.

You compete continually with yourself to make you better.

And if your chief competitor is yourself, you will find that you get along a lot better with everyone else.

CONFESSIONS

Confessions, like urgent telephone calls, are important only to the people who make them.

No matter what she says, she doesn't really want to know the name, address, and measurements of the first girl you made it with.

No matter what she says, she doesn't really want to know what you did to make you an hour late for dinner.

No matter what she says, she doesn't really want to know what your mother and sister think of her.

No matter what she says, she doesn't really want to know if you like that outfit she loves to wear.

Any time you are tempted to confess, stop and think . . . will it make her happier, prouder, more confident, more secure, more lovable, more tolerant of you?

If the answer is no to any of those questions, shut up and keep smiling. After all, wouldn't you rather be accused of a white lie than a black heart?

CONSCIOUSNESS-RAISING

Treating the girls like women is not a sometime thing. You have to think full-time about women and their roles. Edward B. Wilson II, the president of the J. Walter Thompson advertising agency, learned that at his annual meeting in May, 1974, when he reported to shareholders that 10 percent of the vice-presidents in the agency were women. "We have a long way to go," he reported, "but we are making progress, girls."

"Girls?" came a woman's voice from the audience.

CONTENTMENT

Forget it. Never again will we know the contentment that brought Carnation all that milk.

Part of the contentment we've known in the past had an element of sedation in it. Years ago, when "women's lib" was just beginning, a thoughtful young sociologist from California came to see John Mack Carter to tell him that something was happening in men-women relationships, something akin to the civil rights activity that had changed the worlds of black and white.

The sociologist explained that by his calculations women had reached a state of achievement through labor-saving devices and general affluence that would bring about a deep discontent, that with these improvements would come a recognition of the need for still further improvements, and so would continue a never-ending spiral resulting in a massive movement for women's liberation.

John Mack Carter wasn't provoked or puzzled by what Richard Farson told him, but was merely politely conciliatory.

After all, in those days even men who would

later help lead in the fight for sexual equality still wondered what mankind could do for womankind after developing the self-cleaning oven.

CONVENTIONS

Conventions call for conventional attitudes, not a change in personality. If you are Buddy Bashful in the office, no one expects you to be Burt Reynolds or Don Rickles when you get to Conventionland.

Convention wardrobes should also be in keeping with your personality, your life-style, and your body. In warm-weather resort areas most conventioneers are comfortable in slacks, sports shirts, and jackets. If you wear jeans, be sure you are young enough and thin enough to look like you know what you are wearing. If the meeting is in a city like New York, Chicago, or San Francisco, you will be dressed appropriately if you wear your usual business clothes.

Womanizing at conventions is something wives fear—and so do most men. Men at conventions usually end the day at restaurants with other men talking long into the night. Office, not sexual, politics provides the topic of conversation.

All conventioneers, however, should watch their drinking (no one wants to see associates who can't hold their liquor), hours (if the meeting starts at 8 A.M., don't go to bed at 5 A.M.), and calls home (do call and tell her you are lonely and bored because chances are she is).

COOKING

Nobody in his right mind really believes that only men make great chefs. Men's only edge is that they've usually managed to have someone else at elbow cleaning out the strainer and scraping the burned burger from the skillet so they are free to season and taste.

With today's supermarket shelves, anybody can cook. So don't take too much credit for the light and lovely pancakes or the steaks you've scorched and served. The real skill is at the sink. If *you* cook, clean it up.

If *she* cooks, clean it up too, and you'll feel more of a man than you ever imagined.

CRYING

e are told that man is the only animal that laughs. And the only animal that cries. But when was the last time you saw a man crying?

As a matter of fact, man doesn't cry enough. He leaves it to woman, and then complains that she cries too much.

Men are wont to claim that they haven't cried since childhood, because crying supposedly isn't manly. What is this thing about crying, anyway? If it's been that long since you felt like crying, you haven't been living. Even if life is a bowl of cherries, you are bound to hit a few pits along the way. You can either swear a blue streak or you can cry a few tears.

Too many tears have been let in the privacy of the locker room and not enough in public. No real woman is going to think you are less a real man.

Besides, it's better for you than ulcers.

CURBSTONE KISSES

Is there anything that makes you feel more like the first of May than turning a corner and seeing a couple embracing and kissing tenderly? Public display of affection is heartwarming. Demonstrations of mouth-to-mouth resuscitation, however, belong in First Aid class.

Any time you show affection for a woman, it is appreciated by her, and the warmth of your gesture satisfies those who see you. What is embarrassing for onlookers is to be witness to the quick feel, the prodigious poke, the tenderloin touch.

But as for kneesies and touchies . . . well, isn't that why we have two sexes?

DANCING

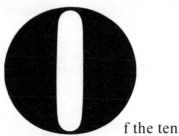

Of the ten thousand books published last year, it seems that at least a thousand of them must have been on the subject of sex. From homo to uni, from over to under. Yet the wise man knows that being an extraordinary sexual partner is as nothing when compared with being an outstanding dancing partner. Even today there aren't too many opportunities to win broad public acclaim for sexual prowess, but a smooth turn around the dance floor will win you the approval of dozens of women and the envy of every stumblebum in the house.

Present yourself promptly at the Twinkletoes Studio tomorrow morning and spend fifty dollars learning your left foot from your right. The result will be far more conquests than you'll ever make with karate lessons.

Remember, no one ever kicked sand in Arthur Murray's face.

DAUGHTERS
(PART I)

In earthier
societies than ours the birth of a daughter may
be greeted openly with disappointment. The real
celebration is accorded the birth of a son because
the young male will contribute the heavy labor
necessary to shelter and feed the family.

Even in our society the birth of a daughter
is sometimes secretly a disappointment to the
father. Yet from this strained beginning can
come the most rewarding of family ties, if you
just let it happen.

But this singular delight also entails a double
responsibility. First, your open affection for your
daughter must be balanced with attention to
your son. And it must be affection that encircles
the rest of the family rather than a circle that
rules them out.

This is especially true regarding the daughter's
attitude toward the mother. There's an easy
temptation to the ego to play the "we against
her" game. It's up to you to keep that from
happening.

Your daughter particularly needs your
encouragement to know that the world outside

the home is her world, too, that your expectation regarding her career and education equals the expectation you have of your son.

She'll still be your daughter for all of her life.

DAUGHTERS (PART II)

hat happens to the protective father/adoring daughter relationship in a liberated era? No matter how old your daughter is, these are some of the things you may have to face and resolve in your changing relationship with her:

1. Her questioning of your values. Once dutiful daughters never argued because Daddy knew best, but now dutiful daughters understand their first duty is to develop themselves, and many wonder how they can do it with an outmoded hand-me-down code of ethics.

    Question: How well can you handle a challenge to your personal value system

. . . and can you plead your case without alienating your daughter? If you cannot do it now, you ought to start working on some good answers.

2. Her relationship to the family. If she earns her own money, does that make her her own woman? Where do responsibility and loyalty to her family come in?

   Question: Can you instill a sense of family in your daughter without making yourself seem hopelessly out-of-date? If not, maybe you had better review your actions before criticizing hers. In other words, Daddy, what have you done for her lately—No, no, put your wallet away—to make her feel loved and loving?

3. Her romantic involvements. Nice girls used to marry the boy next door. But that is not possible anymore because the boy next door is playing guitar on the San Francisco waterfront and your daughter is studying in Switzerland. They will probably never meet, much less marry.

   Question: If you think the new sexual relationships are terrific for you and your friends, can you think the same for your daughter? If not, you'd better go back to square one and recheck those good old values of yours.

DENTISTS

Of all the words of mouth or men, the saddest are these, "Open wide." And of all the misguided matings of professions and sexes, the strangest may well be dentistry. Dental records are kept by the hygienist (female); bills are rendered by the dentist (male).

Our instant x-ray shows a large cavity in the profession: Dental schools need to start seriously recruiting women, for their own good, our well-being, and better dentistry. Since dentists are both doctors and jewelers, and women have a talent in both departments, why not more female dentists?

Male or female, it will hurt for only a minute.

DISCRIMINATION

I f you have ever been discriminated against, you can understand how self-defeating discrimination is, for you know the victim of discrimination is forced to mobilize his energies to fight attacks instead of using his or her talents in positive ways.

There are both subtle and unsubtle discriminatory practices against women, and here are some you may recognize:

1. Economic discrimination. That happens any time a woman is paid less than a man for the same work.
2. Office discrimination. He gets the office with the window, and she gets the office that faces a brick wall.
3. Secretarial discrimination. The personnel office hires only women secretaries.
4. Advancement discrimination. This is an expression of the corporate belief that she's moving too fast in the organization and management knows that women have to take it slower or they will start getting fancy ideas.

5. Partnership discrimination. The ultimate. The company, law firm, or doctors' group that permits only men to enjoy full partnership.

DISHES

Thanks to the miracle of modern advertising, we all now know that washing dishes went out with such obsolete chores as firing the furnace and hanging out the wash. Now the automatic dishwasher does it all.

Not so. Unless you think of your mate as the automatic dishwasher.

Great as the dishwasher is, the world of the modern kitchen is still full of pots and pans and sticky glasses and eggy forks.

Do 'em.

If you already have a good warm feeling inside because after one of the three meals served every day in your house—dinner—you stick around long enough to pick up the dish towel and take a few strokes to dry the things left on the drainboard, and get a "thank you" for that effort, just think what you might get if you seized your share of the responsibility and plunged into the suds up to your elbows, scouring pads and all.

Not just at Thanksgiving either. But after every meal and any time you happen to be passing through the kitchen to dirty a glass or scatter cookie crumbs. Like tonight.

DIVORCE

Most divorce is necessary, but the attendant acrimony is not. Since divorce, like marriage, is dependent on two people, make sure you are doing your part to keep life as unhassled as possible for both of you during a trying time.

If you cannot speak to her without arguing, let your attorney do all the talking for you.

Do not use your children as message carriers, pawns, or excuses at this time.

Do not speak against your wife. You once thought you loved her enough to marry her.

Don't feel guilty.

Divorce is not the end of the world. Sometimes it is the beginning. But it is also the beginning of aloneness and self-sufficiency.

Make sure you have some good friends to see you through the difficult days, because if you do not, you may find yourself back in the same unhappy marriage. Or a new unhappy one.

DOUBLE STANDARD

he double standard is about as old as bathtub gin and just about as satisfying.

If you think it is perfectly all right for men to sleep with willing young women, it has to be all right for women to go to bed with consenting males.

And if you are shocked and dismayed by such sexual conduct on the part of women, you must be equally distraught over the meanderings of men.

In this egalitarian society there really is no room for two sexual attitudes. What is right for men is right for women, and what must be condemned in women must be judged equally wrong in men.

DRINKING

Christian Scientists and members of the WCTU are not the only ones who believe you do not have to drink in order to have a good time. Forcing liquor on unwilling guests (that means in your own home or at a restaurant or a bar) is just plain bad manners. Some people can't drink for a variety of reasons, and you don't have to expose all their private concerns by pushing, pushing, pushing unwanted liquor at them.

On the other hand, some people can't recognize their own limits, but if you are in reasonably good shape you can help, and it's up to you to let the bartender know they've had enough.

Women generally hold liquor less well than men, and this is now believed to be due to the fact that the volume of blood in a woman's body is usually less than that in a man's body. Alcohol is therefore more diluted in a male than in a female.

If you're with a woman, help her be herself; don't let her or encourage her to overindulge.

DRIVING

If your name isn't Andretti or Unser, take your big foot off the gas pedal and move over.

File your woman driver jokes with your old collection of Little Black Sambo stories.

There may have been a time—say, back when the steering wheel of the Essex was made of ash and every trip began by turning the crank at the front of the engine. Maybe. But today's car key responds to the lacquered nail as readily as to the massive fist, and hydraulic lines have replaced back muscles.

As for the massive machinery under the hood and the mysteries thereof known only to men, let's all admit that the automotive engineers have long since passed men by, too.

There are more women drivers than men. They buy most of the gasoline at the pumps. And they are buying a greater percentage of the cars all the time. As for driving abilities, check your insurance company. They were giving women favorable rates when banks were still restricting their credit cards to the husband.

And don't assume you're the driver. Hertz

may have put her in the driver's seat, so if it's her car, go to the left door only to hold it open for the driver.

Still, don't forget your seat belt.

END OF THE AFFAIR

There are maybe 142 good ways to begin an affair but not a single good way to end one. If you are getting bored or disinterested with the woman in your life, then give her some warning.

But do not be too hasty in calling a halt. A man who believed that the woman he was seeing was too possessive for his tastes was about to ask for a change in the relationship, but since her birthday was that week he decided to wait several days. Four days later, when he would have said something, he found he didn't want to say it. He was lucky. You can be smart. Just take a few days to think about Anything Momentous you want to say to a woman.

On the other hand, don't prolong the end. In

the name of kindness men sometimes continue a kind of falling-down relationship that only keeps both partners from continuing their lives in a productive fashion.

The least painful way to end is the most direct. In putting words together be sure you damage her ego as little as possible. After all, you did see something in her. Let her feel she was also responsible for blowing the whistle. In other words, keep her pride intact. And, above all, do not discuss her or her foibles with anyone. The fact that you are out says more than all the words in the world.

EQUALITY OF THE SEXES

It will come about the day someone introduces a dishwashing liquid for men.

FEMININE INTUITION

It's there, men, so listen to it. It's the same intuition that a mother has for a child. It's called caring.

When she feels that something is going to happen, it's because *people* make things happen and women are more interested in people than men are. Helen Gurley Brown learns more things about a new male acquaintance in five minutes than most of his male friends know after five years.

It has nothing to do with sex. It's the things he never got asked, wouldn't think to talk about otherwise. Not how much money he makes, but what he wants his daughter to be when she grows up. Not whether he played football in college, but why Rosemary Lane was his favorite movie star.

And the better you know a person, the more likely you are to have good intuition.

FEMINISTS

So you think the leaders of the women's movement are a bunch of loudmouths, lesbians, and malcontents? Well, some of them are. The most important thing is that you understand that in the forefront of all social reform in every country is the malcontent, the disenfranchised, the citizen with the least to lose. This is true of every movement from child labor to the push for sexual equality.

What you must understand is that not all the women in the movement can be categorized with single statements. The first wave in each social advance is filled with the most vocal supporters, but part of that noise is not volume, but shock. Shock because someone has the derring-do to challenge the establishment.

Today there is a diversity of opinion, talent, and objectives among women. There is no subject women are not exploring for themselves. There is no wall too high to leap, not even a convent wall. There is no bed too warm to leave, not even a long-time marriage bed. And there is no child too protected to understand this is a changing world.

What most women really need from men today is support, emotional support, to continue their search for themselves. They need to find humor and comfort and a sense of worth given by the men in their lives. And when they find that, women—feminists included—are willing to return all the old-fashioned things men want, which means, of course, love in all its forms.

FIRED BY, BEING

Similar semantics to the contrary, firing and being fired have very little in common as forms of saying farewell.

Being fired is always preferable if you can afford the luxury. Being fired by a woman is different and delicate only in that the ax in all likelihood is being handled by a relative amateur. Women executives with firepower weren't all that common when the world was young.

As a matter of conscience-easing, the female boss may have worked herself into a state of hostility for the occasion. Even with the job gone, you still have a lot to lose in this meeting.

Make the job easier for her. Instead of starting a debate, say you are sorry things didn't work out because you felt you were progressing in your work under her direction. However, you accept her move as a business decision; you know she must have the right team. Perhaps she can tell you where you erred so that you won't repeat the mistakes elsewhere. Since you aren't going to undermine her efforts, perhaps she will let you stay on the job for a specified time while you quietly explore other avenues? If she grants this, it's worth more than severance. Because the best way to get a new job is to have an old one.

FIRING

Firing a woman is really no different from firing a man. Here there truly is equality.

Since no one likes to fire anyone, you have to think about it long before it happens, wishing it would go away. Then you promise yourself you will do it on Friday. But you don't want to spoil her weekend, so you let the day slip away and spoil your own instead, waiting for another week. Then when your stomach is in total disarray and you can't go another night without sleep, you call her in and do the deed. And there are no tears or tantrums or other differences except that women seem to take firing with more grace than men. Perhaps women know that personal animosity or jealousy is rarely involved. And they suspect they will go on to better things.

If you can see any real benefit in explaining the firing, take the time to specify the mismatch of job requirements with talents, with the hope that she can learn something that will make her more effective next time. If a review isn't truly constructive, though, and involves faults that can't be corrected, leave her personal dignity intact.

Remember, as you probably would for a man, that you have a responsibility to help toward the next job. In addition to the severance benefits stiffly outlined in the personnel manual (which proves so useless at this time of need), offer office space, the telephone, use of the secretarial pool, and any other services. It won't bankrupt the company.

Not that you won't be held personally responsible by the woman involved. From now on. But you will feel better about doing what you had to do. By the way, did you *really* have to? Would you have fired the "person" if she were he?

Finally, it may just be that you are removing a woman because you think the job has to be done by a man. If this is so, you must be reading this book with the TV tuned to the ball game.

FLIRTING

Now is the time to forget everything you learned in high school and college about flirting. It's more a habit than anything else, and as tough to break as having a cigarette with your coffee.

The lingering smile, the wink, the passing pat, the arm around the waist—all are forms of a promise you don't mean. In business enough promises you really intend to honor get broken without adding the one that has the suggestion of sexual exploration later.

A new golden rule: don't flirt unless you are serious about carrying through with it. Right between the sheets. Are you that serious? Face it, if you are making plans that lead to bed it isn't likely to be the receptionist you will have to say hello to for many mornings to come.

Besides, don't you really think she can do better at any singles bar?

But if you can't be cured from flirting, how about cutting down?

FLYING

Something about flying brings out the chauvinist in the most sensible businessman. Perhaps there is a symbolic separation from reality that somehow so separates a man from his senses that he becomes the instant jester. Just remember, whatever the wisecrack or proposition, your stewardess has heard it before, from a thousand other men on a hundred other flights from Pittsburgh to Paducah. Just put the seat belt around your tongue and remember:

1. The airlines are in the transportation business, not the entertainment business. You paid for a trip, not an experience.
2. If you want to complain about the food, call the airline and not the stewardess. All airline food is made of congealed spare parts. The "stew" didn't cook it.
3. Don't ask her to break the rules for you by serving coffee on take-off or more drinks than allowed in the air.
4. Don't touch. She walks by you dozens of times and can't reach the overhead

racks without stretching over you. But it's a job to her. Remember, she didn't write the ad that says "Fly Me," or personally make the promise, "We move our tail for you."

5. Don't jump up when the plane lands and crowd the aisle in violation of her repeated instructions. One of these days some stewardess is going to flip and dump you out the emergency chute. You've probably earned it.

6. Remember to be nice to her; she does not always get equal treatment from the airline. Some airlines provide meals only for the flight crew. Stewards and stewardesses get meals only if passengers have leftovers or don't order their meal.

7. If you really want to give a "stew" a treat, surprise her by remembering her name. It won't get you her telephone number or an offer of more than coffee, tea, or milk, but the smile will be genuine.

FREEDOM

The free or liberated woman is the one who causes consternation these days, because the old-style "you ask me first" woman knows the man is always the chaser and the woman is always the chasee.

For this woman the rules are simple, and freedom is simply the right to say no.

But for less repressed women, women who are truly free, the right to pursue is also part of freedom.

It does mean that women can make the first call and invite him to lunch. It does mean that a woman can extend an invitation to a dinner party or the theater. It does mean that nice women can invite nice men before nice men call them.

Does freedom mean only pursuit of a man?
Of course not.

It also means pursuit of a career, pursuit of legal social reform . . . and pursuit of happiness.

FRIENDS, BUSINESS

 woman in
your business can be one of your best friends if
you both will let it happen. Because men and
women do have different insights and
perceptions, because they do have different
frames of reference and experience, they can
counsel each other in unique ways.

It is particularly helpful to be friendly with
women at your level of business. They can help
you see through some of the daily problems and
personalities you deal with.

The best way to befriend a woman in business
is with the business lunch. Cocktails can have a
non-business meaning; dinner is something
wives want. Speaking of dinner, it is generally
good form to avoid cozy little foursomes that
include his wife and her husband. It strains a
relationship that isn't meant to be social; its real
value is at the nine-to-five level.

FRIENDS, SOCIAL

It is comforting, rewarding, fulfilling to have a best-friend relationship with someone of the opposite sex. If that person is also your mate, it is even better. The advantages of any male-female friendship, however, are many.

Such a friendship is rarely, if ever, tinged with jealous overtones, and advice given is tendered with the other person's welfare in mind.

Anyone who has ever read a psychology book knows that the first rule in friendship is to like one's self and feel worthy of friendship, but it is a lot easier to like one's self when you notice other people like you, too.

The most difficult thing in male-female friendships is to avoid the usual sexist pitfalls (like falling in love or antagonizing the persons who love you and your friend). And the most important thing to do to nurture the friendship is to allow yourselves some real time to develop together . . . to talk, to share experiences, to truly know one another.

FUTURE PROFESSIONALS

The honor and profit of the professions have belonged almost exclusively to men in this country. But now the spoils are about to be divided. The M.D.s and L.L.B.s of tomorrow are the Ms. and Mrs. of today.

In the first-year classes in law schools and medical schools today 22 percent and 23 percent respectively are women.

Is this remarkable increase the result of favoritism as a remedy for past discrimination? No way. On the medical school admissions tests, the female candidates matched the men point for point. For law school admissions, women managed to score slightly higher than the men.

When you hang out your shingle today, it comes in the color of your choice.

GETTING
TO KNOW HER

There is a very wealthy man in Dallas who, whenever he meets a woman he'd like to know better, flies her to his house in Acapulco or his house on the Riviera or has her delivered by helicopter to his Wyoming ranch. Once she's there, he proceeds to get to know her. You would think that with such careful screening and such nice prizes to offer he would win over any woman in the world.

But, women being what they are, it doesn't work that way. This man has managed to pick three wrong women for wives, uncounted wrong women for mistresses, and has survived about six hundred rotten weekends.

To a Woman of Worth, a man's net worth is not the most important thing in the world. In the early days of a relationship, the discovery of shared values is the first major breakthrough. And if you really want to get to know her, then concentrate on putting together some real time that gives you both the chance to share the values you talk about.

Don't just talk about art. Visit the museums.

Don't just read the reviews. See the play (film, ballet, etc.).

Don't just press your nose against the bakery window. Bake your own bread.

If you really want to get to know a woman, you will have to run the risk of letting her get to know you.

GIFTS

There isn't a female secretary alive who hasn't assumed that it is part of her duty to do almost all the gift buying for her boss. The bosses haven't had to be pushed. She buys the business gifts and selects birthday and Christmas gifts for his wife and/or his girl friend.

Certainly this arrangement contradicts the adage that it is not the gift but the thought that counts.

Starting now, shop for the gifts yourself. If it means you have to cut down the number you buy, probably so much the better. You might even learn your wife's dress size and other enlightening data.

When you send your secretary for a gift, make it her own.

GOING PLACES

There is another term for the woman who is going places. It is called achiever. In the business world there are two kinds of people: those who achieve and those who don't care about going places.

Men who are achievement-oriented really do not have too many hang-ups about who and what they are. Women, on the other hand, still fall into the old trap of woman achiever in conflict with sexual woman. Who is she? What is her identity? Is she really a womanly woman?

Women are concerned that their business success will come at the expense of the female side of themselves. Can they retain their femininity and their pension and welfare?

If you are involved in business or in your social life with a woman achiever, there are certain things you can do to reinforce her image of herself. One, of course, is to be a good listener when she needs a man to talk to. Another is to remind her that you are aware of the feminine side of her. And the third and most important is to avoid creating situations that continually force evaluation and reevaluation of her life role so that she is made to feel guilty, unworthy, and rejected.

GOSSIP

hat do you mean by gossip?

Just the idle talk and groundless rumors that all of us make about people.

What do you mean by all of us?

Just what we said—all of us. Men and women.

Aren't women the ones who do all the gossiping, though?

Oh, come on now. What about the man in the locker room who tells you about the club member who picks up golf balls? What about the man who tells you about the tennis partner who miscalls shots? What about the conversation in the bar about the next man to get the company presidency? What about the talk going around about the new girl in the sales department?

Business and sexual practices make for plenty of gossip by men. The best thing you can do about gossip is not indulge in it. The second best thing you can do is ignore it when it is brought to you.

HAIRCUTS, NEW DRESSES, AND OTHER REASONS FOR MEN'S OPINIONS

It does not matter if she is curly, straight, fluffed, or puffed. Think twice before you tell her what you think her beauty shop appointment has done for her. It is one thing to criticize a dress she can change; it is quite another thing to say you hate her short hair (what should she do—buy a wig or hunch her shoulders to make her hair look long?).

Women have a rare understanding with the people who cut, set, blow dry, color, and otherwise change their hair. And since we already know that women are more sensitive about their hair than they ever were about their teen-age acne, you had better be sensitive, too.

Before you say what you honestly think, decide whether she can easily change what you dislike. In other words, it's perfectly all right to tell her that you don't like her hair turned up . . . you like it turned under. It's fine to like her hair color with more red or less green or a touch of turquoise—all those things can be done. But you can't easily uncurl a curly look, and while a haircut can be edited, it can't be the way it was before the appointment.

When it comes to her clothes, you can be more critical, depending on the time and place. If you know the occasion is important to her, be sure to tell her you like the way she looks. Find something believable to tell her about her appearance. It will buoy her and, like you, she needs the confidence. Never tell a woman you don't like her dress *after* you have arrived at the meeting, the party, or the Important Event. If her slip shows, tell her before she leaves the house. If you wish she wouldn't go braless, don't wait until she is standing before twelve hundred gawking people to tell her. You don't have to lie about the way a woman looks; you just have to pick the right time and place to lay on the criticism.

If her manners, politics, religion, buck teeth, or accent bug you, you ought to stop seeing her. There are some things a woman can't change. Not even for you.

HANDY PERSONS

She wants a tool kit for Christmas and a power saw for her birthday.

Is she crazy?

No. She's just doing what she can to make life easier for everybody. So don't laugh when she reaches for a hammer instead of a ham. And don't worry about her femininity. Any woman who can save the price of a plumber is worth her weight in power tools.

HER DOG, CAT, PARAKEET, AND/OR PLANTS

Remember when they used to say, "Love me, love my dog"? Well, you don't have to love her dog, but you should offer to walk it on occasional rainy nights. You ought to make friends with her cat. You might try to smile at her parakeet. And definitely learn to talk to her plants.

None of these things guarantees the romance, of course, but when you do something nice for someone or something a woman loves, her gratitude is wondrous to behold. And women can be very imaginative when it comes to saying thank you.

HOUSEGUESTS

Living with somebody usually comes down to her business and yours. But when you decide to be the houseguests of members of your family, the question of who sleeps where does arise.

If you and your woman are visiting parents (yours or hers) and they know you live together, they should have no objection to your staying together. The assumption, of course, is that they also have no objection to your living together.

If there are grandparents in the home who are not aware of your sleeping arrangements, plan to sleep in separate rooms when you go home. Grandparents, generally, are not able to make the transition from their generation to yours without reaching for the smelling salts.

If there are younger brothers and sisters in the home and the parents are concerned about your living arrangements, accommodate them and sleep solo.

Living together is a personal thing, but when you ask other people to offer their hospitality, you are required to give up your individual desires if they are in conflict with the majority.

In other words . . . you can go home again. But must you make waves?

HOUSEWIVES

Cool it, mister. It isn't such a terrible thing to be. (What did *your* mother do?) The only housewives to scorn are those who are themselves contemptuous of the role. Sure, the world is changing, but that does not mean that every woman has to go out and get a job. There are some women who would rather stay home and fill the traditional job of homemaking. As long as a woman is doing what she wants to do, she is a contemporary woman. If she wants to stay home and make apple pies and babies, it does not mean she is rejecting the world. What it really means is that she is contributing to it.

IMAGES

emember when all women wore pillbox hats and sleeveless dresses and tried to look like Jackie Kennedy? Well, it is not like that anymore.

That means you can throw away your formula (as well as your ideal measurement list as found in *Playboy, Penthouse,* and *Viva)* because women are individuals now.

Do not judge women by group standards.

Do not expect "feminine characteristics," but look instead for those qualities that make a woman her own person.

By the way, this lack of universal image works in your favor, too.

It means you do not have to be Robert Redford or even Paul Newman. And it means you are allowed to let your emotions hang out without having women or other men shake their heads sadly and say, "Poor Max. He's no John Wayne."

INDIVIDUALITY

ou cannot
generalize about women any more than you can
about football players, Siamese cats . . . or men.
And most particularly you cannot generalize
when it comes to liberated women.

All liberated women are not alike. They do not
all spend their time attending rallies, marching
in long forgotten protest groups, or writing
belligerent letters to the editors of left-wing
papers.

The woman who is truly liberated is the one
who has her own life-style. She is the woman
who is doing what she really wants to do with her
life. Instead of sitting-in on her free evenings, she
may be sitting down to do needlepoint and
watch television.

Liberation has been with us a long time, but
we didn't know what to call it. Golda Meir, Mrs.
Vijaya Pandit, Madame de Staël, Margaret
Mead—all of them are liberated women who by
example have made it possible for other women
to create themselves in their reflected image.

So if you are really looking for liberated
women, stay out of parades. Liberated women

are more likely to be loners and individualists, and while some things may scare these women about their lives, some things make them very secure.

INSECURITY

f all the insecurities suffered by males, perhaps the most grievous is economic insecurity. Under the pretense of "Women don't have the stamina for this job," or "I wouldn't want my sister to work like this," is the unspoken but always present issue of job security.

During World War II, when men were called to service, it was found that women could, would, and did, replace males in factories and in other heavy labor situations. But when the war ended everybody went to the movies, and America was once again assured that when a girl gave up her job for a boy she found happiness. Even after the war career women melted happily into the arms of weak men before the final fade-out. And then television came along to promise all the wives (through series after series of dull-witted situation comedies) that Smart

Mom could fool Dear Old Dad seven ways to Sunday.

So here we are, all of us, victims of media brainwash. We are still willing to believe that women don't belong in certain areas of life, but what most of us are really saying is that we do not want women to compete economically with men.

That is a painful admission, but until you are able to make it, you will have a hard time adjusting to women in business. Once you recognize the insecurity you can overcome it, because the first step in problem solving is always recognition of the problem.

IN SICKNESS AND –

There are two things never to do when a woman is sick:

1. Don't hover, and
2. Don't go to Las Vegas

The body anxieties of men are monumental, and when a man is ill, every woman knows he is certain The End is near. Women realize that men have a lower pain tolerance than women, and furthermore, men simply do not expect to be sick. Therefore, every sniffle is a terminal cold, and every hangnail is a possible malignancy.

If you are sick, give in and go to bed with a moan and a whimper. But don't drag around telling everyone in your office and home how sick you are.

Or else they will tell you how sick they are . . . of your complaints.

INTERVIEWING

O kay. So there are two women you are interviewing for the job. One is terrific looking, dresses well, and all her equipment is in place. The other is a refugee from a Weight Watchers class. How do you interview them?

One boss interviewed them in the following ways:

The Pretty Woman Interview. He spent twenty minutes saying, "Gee, you're pretty. I mean you're really pretty. Where did you go to school? Boy, are you pretty!" He hired her without knowing if she could spell her name.

The Fat Woman Interview. He spent two hours interviewing her about everything from her education to the books she read, the TV programs she watched, and the political causes she espoused. At the end of that time and after a test project she completed with high honors, he hired her.

The two women worked in the same department, and when the pretty woman found out about the second woman's interview, she was chagrined. As the result of the ways in which they were interviewed, the first woman has never been given a challenging assignment, although her qualifications and talents equal those of the second woman. The boss was so impressed with the pretty woman he couldn't believe she did anything but twirl a baton.

INTRODUCTIONS

e'll assume you read Emily Post and learned that there is a formula for introducing people. ("Miss Jones, I'd like you to meet Mr. Williams.")

The formula still works, by the way. But introductions have become a lot more complicated. The introductions that concern us are business introductions.

Should a man stand when a woman comes

into his office? Only if he stands when a man comes into his office. For example, a person visiting an office for the first time, whether male or female, should be greeted by a host who rises for him or her.

Should formal etiquette be pursued in a meeting? No. The most convenient kind of introductions should be made. For example, when three or more people are being introduced they can be introduced as they stand, left to right. Expediency without any discourtesy is the rule of thumb.

Should wives be introduced when businessmen meet at dinner? Always. If she's there, she has to be acknowledged with more than a smile and a nod.

JEALOUSY, PROFESSIONAL

You don't intend to let it happen, but suddenly there it is: just a slight twinge when Sally, who works two notches below you, is advanced, a deeper pang when your wife's salary goes ahead of yours, and an unmistakable wrench when you move back two steps while a woman takes your place.

How do you handle professional jealousy?

First, by improving your own skills so that you increase your confidence, for awareness of growth is one of the things that makes us all feel better about ourselves.

Second, by carefully analyzing the reasons for the other person's business success. Does she work harder? Longer? Is she really better to begin with? Answer the questions honestly. You'll be more secure if you do.

Third, if you really think she got where she is because of her bod, not her mind, get out. And find a job (or marriage) where your security is not threatened by unreasonable sexual pressure.

You see, being a woman doesn't always work against women. Sometimes it works against men.

JEALOUSY, SEXUAL

f she is so liberated, why is she so jealous?

Because, you crazy man, you made her that way.

You took all that stuff about open marriage as a license to hunt, and she is hurt.

You figured the new sexual freedom was

meant just for you, so you told her about your conquests.

You reached for her in bed and said, "Gwen, darling," but her name is Phyllis.

You could not take your eyes or your hands off the new girl you met at some old party, and her friends are still talking about it.

In short, you took away the emotional support and let her think she was unloved and unwanted. You behaved like an irresponsible man, so she is acting like a hurt woman.

What you really have to remember is that the emotions will be the last part of all of us to be liberated.

JEKYLL AND HYDE

**M**ost businessmen today tend to be two-faced without even knowing it. They live almost equally in two totally separate worlds, the office and the home. Because responsibilities and pressures seem so different in each world, they unconsciously tend to assume a different role for each. Alec Guinness' ferryboat paradise had aspects familiar to every man.

When you put on your vest, you put on an

office image that makes you fair-minded, quick to reward, and slow to anger.

When the vest comes off, it leaves you a churl who growls at the dog and complains about the toast.

Be fair. Spread some of your pettiness around the office. Or, if you really prefer to be all sweetness and light, try a little sunshine with the slippers.

KISSING

Even though movies and books have changed, there is something that Clark Gable did and Faith Baldwin wrote about that still works. It is called kissing. In a world where orgasm and sexual deviation seem to be the only things worth talking about, it is important to remember that kissing is still one of the things worth doing.

You can kiss a woman for a lot of reasons, but almost without exception a kiss makes a woman feel wanted, protected, maybe even a little fragile.

The best time to kiss a woman is when she least expects it. The little peck on the cheek for each hello and good-bye is hardly worth remembering, much less explaining. The kisses that matter are the kisses that come from the heart, the impromptu once-in-a-while kisses that women use to light the fire of memory.

It does not have to be a kiss that is loaded with technique and sexual overtones. The best kiss is one that is given with love, and love really is the kind of thing you can feel for almost anyone at certain special times. Don't go around kissing the world. It's boring.

Save your kisses . . . and who knows? She may not be the only one remembering them with warmth and delight.

LABOR-SAVING DEVICES

Until recently the most significant labor-saving device ever developed for man was woman. Then along came dishwashers (to replace a husband in the kitchen) as well as mixers, waxers, washers, dryers, ovens (self-cleaning and otherwise), and a slew of other twentieth-century marvels. In their rush to be liberated from guilt feelings, a lot of men have bought a lot of women many work-saving devices.

But what men do not realize—or stop to ask—is

whether women really want those work-saving devices.

One housewife in Duluth said, "If he buys me a floor waxer, I will leave him. I got by for seventeen years without a floor waxer, and if he puts one in the house, I'll feel compelled to use it—and hate him every minute."

The mate of a man in Rochester said, "He bought me a washer-dryer combination and changed my life. Now I can't send things out to the laundry. Now I spend two hours a week with my washer-dryer instead of at the tennis court. I am going to run an ad this weekend and sell the stupid thing."

So next time you are tempted to buy a woman a labor-saving device, make sure it is also guaranteed to save relationships.

LANGUAGE

The language of business is filled with more than "contract," "annuity," "pension and welfare." Men have spent so much time in business together that they have developed a four-letter-word locker room shorthand for most things they want to say, and the advent of women in the meeting room is putting some males at a loss for words. Men must understand that women really have heard all those ugly, nasty words before. What is more, many women today use them. Locker room language is a lazy way of talking. There are perfectly acceptable Anglo-Saxon words that convey despicable action, unpardonable deeds, and poor performance. So why shouldn't everyone, men and women, learn to use them?

We are in danger of becoming a four-letter country, and that is an indication of our unwillingness to think, to make the effort to express ourselves adequately, and, by so doing, re-sort our thoughts and actions. It is also another reflection of the lack of discipline in our lives.

Just one thing, however. Don't overdo the language number. Unless you were born before 1900, you do not have to say "Excuse me" to a woman when you say damn or hell during a meeting.

LAYOFFS

In a year of recession, stagflation, and other economic ills, women are apt to see their job gains reduced. Because they know the old adage "last hired, first fired," many women in troubled industries expect to find themselves job hunting.

Private industry, however, has a responsibility and a commitment to equal opportunity employment. There must be some regard for percentages rather than the easy business of chopping from the bottom of the employment list.

So believes Lynne Darcy of NOW, who says, "Layoffs should be equitable. If white males make up 90 percent of the work force, because of obvious reasons, then certainly they will be harder hit. But I propose if there is to be, say, a 10 percent layoff that the 10 percent come from each group instead of from those with the least seniority, because these would be the last hired—women and minorities."

Still others concerned with the problems of minorities recommend the four-day work week.

But on one thing all agree: the hard-won gains of the past ten years must not be permitted to die in an unemployment line.

LIBERATION

Don't worry; this is not going to be a speech on equality and other ear-splitting, bell-ringing subjects. No word is more overworked and less understood.

103

Liberation is what a lot of people think women expect to have handed them on a silver platter. But it just isn't so. Liberation is not something that can be given to a woman. It is something she must find for herself.

If you are a liberated male, it won't bother you that a woman wants her freedom. And that's about as much as you can do in liberating a woman: just let her know it's okay with you.

Liberation is not a group effort. Liberation is what each woman does to assure her freedom. Liberation is an individual action; it has nothing to do with bra burnings, marches, or symposiums. While all of those may have some significance for women who need to feel that the majority is with them, actual liberation is done in the light of day and the cool of the evening when a woman loosens the bonds of outmoded belief and lets herself breathe.

If the woman in your life is liberated, then hallelujah!—liberation is here. If the woman in your life (or you) is not liberated, then it doesn't matter if she goes braless and you go shoeless as you march around all the swimming pools in Westchester County and Beverly Hills.

The road to liberation is a lonely one, and it isn't lined with coffee klatches and frustrated graduates who refuse to be secretaries. It is lined with typewriters (to be used by both men and women), computers (to be used by same), and keys to executive washrooms (his and hers).

LISTENING

Somewhere along the way men remember to stop and look, but few listen.

The best thing that men and women who love one another can do for each other is listen—and listen with care.

It is insulting to a woman to have a man ask their Saturday night plans after he has been informed three times. It is disappointing to have a man ask if she has ever been to Italy, and only ten minutes after she did her whole Italian number.

But listening between men can be improved, too. It is frustrating to have an employee ask what you thought of the new idea for plant economy when you were the one who suggested it. And if you failed to listen when your boss asked you to collect data on pension and welfare, you may end up collecting unemployment instead.

LOVE

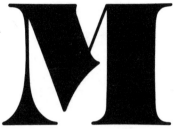

ost men know nothing about love. They know a lot about "relationships," casual affairs, and how to pick up females at bus stops. But they know nothing about the fundamentals of love. And until a man knows how to love a woman he might as well continue bowling and beer with the boys.

If you love a woman . . .

1. You want her to be part of all your life—and you tell her so.
2. You think about dumb ways to please her (like picking up towels from the bathroom floor), and you do them.
3. You let her know when she makes you feel good—and you tell her again and again.
4. You let her know when she makes you feel bad—and you tell her once.
5. You understand that all sexual adjustments are not hers to make—it still takes two satisfactions to make one love.
6. You give her your loyalty and support whether it is in front of her boss, your mother, the children, or some other woman.

106

7. You make no demands you would not answer.
8. About once a day you manage to come right out and say "I love you" in English, Sanskrit, or Morse code.

LOVE AND OTHER INFIDELITIES

More evil is committed in the name of love than any other emotion. And of all the things we feel for one another, love is still the most difficult to recognize, the hardest to define.

At what point do you really know if you love her enough to give her a commitment? And what is a commitment, anyway?

A commitment, sir, begins the minute you say, "I love you," and it lasts until you say, "I leave you."

And the commitment is that you will look after her. If she loves you, then the commitment is mutual, and she accepts her responsibility and will look after you.

Since liberation there has been some question about what "looking after" really means. We define looking after as the actions necessary to insure the emotional and physical well-being of the person you love. There is no division as to his responsibilities in love and hers. There are simply their responsibilities.

The commitment to love is not necessarily a commitment to marriage, living together, or anything legal and binding. It is non-legal and therefore more binding.

LOVING TRAITS

pening car doors is not the be-all and end-all in a contemporary relationship, but it still helps make a woman feel a man is concerned about her. If you believe that loving is caring, then those things you do that show you care are probably your best investment in a shared future.

Some of those loving, sharing traits are found in a man who

1. Is nice to her mother, father, and assorted relatives.
2. Treats her children by previous marriage(s) well.

3. Does not expect her to cook like the French Chef after a day of working like an Egyptian Slave.
4. Never says, "I told you so," "If only you had . . ." "Why don't you?"
5. Tells her she is pretty even if she is liberated.
6. Laughs a lot, at her jokes as well as his own.
7. Surprises her (pleasurably) from time to time.
8. Doesn't criticize her investments.
9. Considers her advice whether or not he asks for it.
10. Doesn't ask what her clothes or furniture cost.
11. Takes or gives money with equal aplomb.
12. Pays back promptly when he borrows.
13. Helps her maintain a civilized relationship with her ex-husband.
14. Doesn't compare her, at least openly, with other women he has loved.
15. Never asks about her previous affairs, marriages, liaisons.
16. At least once every few weeks makes her feel like a mistress if she is a wife, or . . .
17. Makes her feel like a wife if she is a mistress.

MACHO MAN

 omen still want men who are brawny enough to move a sofa, brave enough to attack a spider, and brilliant enough to read the instructions on an assemble-it-yourself furniture kit.

What bugs a woman is the man who—because he is a man—

- Cannot ask directions at a gas station even though you have been driving in circles for two hours
- Insists on shoveling the snowy driveway even though he has done nothing more strenuous than dial a telephone for two years
- Lifts the hood of the car as if he knows what to look for
- Swims too far
- Drinks too much
- Drives too fast
- Takes one chance too many

MADAME

She may look old enough, hennaed enough, or French enough to have you call her Madame.

But don't.

Madame is a small American effrontery, an extension of pretension.

So call her Miss, call her Ms., call her Doctor, or call her by her given name.

But don't call her Madame.

MAKING ALLOWANCES

Judge a woman just like a man.

If you make allowances for his sloppiness, better do the same for hers.

If you know his wife will mop up the floor with him if he leaves after 5:15 P.M., and you live with his curfew, better live with hers.

If you put up with his mean temper, you'd better be able to stand hers without saying, "Got your period, hon?" All ill temper doesn't depend on the calendar. Some of it just might be due to you.

MARRIAGE

In this highly liberated age we understand premarital sex, divorce, abortion, homosexuality, and adultery. The one thing we have difficulty understanding is marriage.

Yet marriage has not changed as much as some people think. What has changed is our expectations of marriage.

Marriage is still based on old-fashioned ideas like loyalty and devotion and faithfulness and cooperation and a desire to share one's destiny with another.

What has happened, of course, is that we are living longer than our great-grandparents, and our joint destinies are getting too joined for some.

We are all very complicated. We are all very confused. We all want to find some kind of relationship, some magic key to one another.

Is that key marriage? Maybe yes. Maybe no.

One thing is certain. Marriage is not perfect. It is not the only way people can live in harmony, but it is the way most people can live in comfort.

Marriage is the ultimate commitment, and liberation (women's or anyone else's) is meaningless unless there is some kind of commitment.

If married is the way you want to live, then treat your partner with courtesy, respect, and tenderness. If you are incapable of doing that with the woman who shares your name, your home, and probably your children, then end the marriage. Because it really isn't very much of a marriage anyway.

And when it comes to marriage, no marriage at all is better than half a marriage.

MARRY, WHEN NOT TO

Everyone does not have to be married, yet some people still continue to make the marriage commitment for all the wrong reasons. There are hundreds of wrong reasons, and these are just a few.

So keep your eyes open, and don't get married if the reasons are that

1. You are escaping from your family.
2. All your friends are married, and you want to be like your friends.
3. You hate the Chinese laundry.
4. You think you ought to be a father.
5. You need someone to talk to (remember, a psychiatrist is cheaper).
6. You like her sister better.
7. You aren't sure you love her, but you think you may learn. (P.S. You won't.)

MEASUREMENTS

For those of you who've long suspected that men are prejudiced by physical attractiveness in hiring women, you're right. For example, when you read the title of this page, did you assume the title referred to corporal dimensions and not measurements of intelligence or skills?

Fortunately personnel departments have become vastly more sophisticated in their hiring tests and can scientifically judge emotional makeup as well as aptitude. But when these tests are handed to the boss to make the final selection, he may still give the job to the blonde in the tight blue sweater.

Unless he is in the business of hiring models, there is no surer way to buy trouble.

MILLIONAIRES

If you are one, don't mention it. It isn't that she isn't interested. It is just that men with money often have a habit of letting the whole world know. You don't have to knock her out with a list of the clubs you belong to. You don't have to overwhelm her with your offices in every country in the world. It is true that power fascinates, but using it as bait is unattractive.

So sit back and let somebody else tell her what a big fish she landed.

MISTRESS

She used to be the woman he kept, but nowadays she probably pays her own rent and may earn as much or more than he. Mature men no longer look for women who want to attach themselves; they much prefer women who are people. Just as mistresses have changed, so have some of the rules:

1. Discretion. It's not necessary in a lot of cases because the thinking of people today accommodates a variety of living arrangements, only one of which is a man and woman not married to one another.

2. Meeting the family. A no-no for a married man with a woman friend. Women who love should be spared the discomfort of making small talk with His Wife, a woman she hates before she meets.

3. Vacations. Take them with her when you can. When you can't, don't show her the slides . . . especially the ones with your wife in a bikini.

4. Holidays. If you're not there, make sure you call her. If you are married, you

117

have to be doubly sure she feels pampered, cherished, worthwhile—all the things a second-place woman is concerned about.
5. Marry her. Or stop talking about it, for God's sake.

MONEYMAKERS

ost men need no instruction in dealing with wives or mates who make less money than they do. But what happens when she contributes the lion's share?

There is really nothing more damaging to a relationship than pretense. If it is her money they are spending, and he acts like a Prussian general taking charge of every decision, there is going to be deep resentment. Difficult as it may be for some to accept, she has the right to veto major money decisions even if her money is *not* a major factor in their income.

Money is as emotional a subject as children and in-laws.

If a couple decides to live on his salary and

bank hers (or vice versa), it makes a good, clean division of moneys and causes less frustration.

But if he abdicates money responsibilities and lets her pay the bills (without a fund, a mutual allowance, or other fiscal arrangement), then he also gives up his rights to decide how the money will be spent.

Once you agree on saving/spending ratios the best thing you can do is set up separate checking accounts so each person has the freedom to buy without cautious editing by his mate.

MOODS

She bites her lips and fights back tears. And when you ask what's wrong, she says tersely, "Nothing."

She hasn't had anything to drink except a diet soda, but she is flirty and flighty and so intoxicatingly enchanting you can't keep your eyes off her.

Both women are in the middle of a mood, and it is just as hard to handle the hyper-happy as it is to deal with a blue lady.

In each case, however, the sensitive man will

deal with—and not ignore—the psychodramas of the woman in his life.

Although the woman who is despondent may seem to resist all offers of understanding, she is in truth crying out for help. You can reach her with affection, interest, and attention. Turn off the TV and turn to her. Put down the magazine so she won't feel put down. Give her all your attention. Zero in. Focus on her, and give her the opportunity to unleash her anger, get rid of her hostility. If she works for you, give her an opportunity to talk to you privately in your office. One insurance executive, aware that his secretary seemed to be increasingly diffident, called her into his office. "Martha, you and I always had a lot of respect for one another, but lately I sense something troubling you. Am I responsible for the change?"

"Of course not," she said in a voice that registered thirty-two degrees below zero.

Because he was smart enough to know that cold answers were hot clues he continued his line of questioning. "Do you feel you make enough money?"

"Enough *in* my job," she said bitterly.

"Oh?" He registered surprise. "And outside your job?"

"I don't work outside."

He knew the rest of the story in minutes. Several women in the office were moonlighting, getting others to cover for them, and as a loyal employee, Martha resented the duplicity around her.

Fortunately her boss did, too, and after he called an end to the moonlighting, he and Martha found that they had an even better employer-employee relationship because he proved he was a man of action, a man she could respect.

In the case of a woman on an emotional high, keep a steadying hand on her. What goes up must come down. If you are there and willing to communicate, you can make her descent comfortable for you both.

MOVIES

hen the movies stopped having sappy, happily-ever-after endings and started dealing with real live people, it not only shook up a lot of older people but it gave all men and women new topics of conversation and new areas to agree and disagree in.

If her taste in film runs to Swedish directors, and you are still happiest with Disney movies, don't go to the movies together. One of you will always be disappointed.

On the other hand, if you both enjoy wallowing in the same kind of movie misery, do so together. But don't feel that she is a Neanderthal woman if she doesn't interpret the film the way you do. And don't let her accuse

you of being a clod if you believe Ingmar
Bergman meant something she doesn't see at all.

Since the price of admission is high these days,
it is perfectly fine to split expenses at the movies.
And it is all right for her to take you. It is also the
courteous thing for the person who arrives at the
theater first to stand in line and get the tickets. In
movies, as in all life these days, convenience is
the new courtesy.

MS.

Not since Colonel
Bertie McCormick converted the *Chicago
Tribune* to phonetic spelling (pardon us, fonetic)
and Dizzy Dean introduced his
four-and-a-half-letter word "ain't" to the public
airways has there been so much ado about so
little: Ms. Those of us who were still trying to
correct our slovenly Southern enunciation found
it strange to be saying Miz again, especially to
single women. Women themselves objected to it
as unnecessary, as Mrs. and Miss seemed to
cover every case.

This certainly was John Mack Carter's initial
feeling when he ruled "Ms." out of the women's

magazine he edited at the time. But he put his readers to a vote on it anyway, and they backed up his decision by objecting to its use four to one.

Strangely enough, some of the most vociferous objections to "Ms." have come from some newspapers, although its use would make their problem of identifying subjects in their news columns much simpler. Maybe they refused because it doesn't appear in their stylebooks.

"Shit" doesn't appear in most of their stylebooks either, but Watergate brought it to the columns of their family newspapers.

It is now time to put humans above the rules and return to every woman her own name. If she wants to be called Ms., do it and get on with the agenda.

"MY GIRL"

No appellation is more offensive than the boss's reference to his secretary as "my girl."

"My girl will make the lunch reservations."

"My girl will get the coffee."

Why is it offensive? Because "my girl" is a refusal to see a woman as an individual. "My girl" has a name, and she wants it used just as much as "my boss" does.

NAME CALLING

Don't give her pet names in business. Honeys, Dolls, and Sweethearts went out with gangster movies in the thirties.

If you're alone with a woman and you love her, it doesn't matter what you call her . . . so long as it pleases her. But when you see her in business, don't treat her like a piece of merchandise. She isn't your honey. You can't take this doll home. And you're not her sweetheart.

Stay away from cutesy-poo names. Women think those names are a put-down. (So do aware men.) A television salesman calls a woman producer "The Soft One." She doesn't call him anything. That is because she does not speak to him. Nor do any of the other women at the station. He calls each of them "The Soft One," too.

NEEDS

The best way to get what you need is to tell a woman.

It is not dirty, smutty, or vulgar to let the woman you love know your sexual needs. There is nothing wrong in verbalizing your desires. In fact, there isn't any reason not to tell any woman who is going to bed with you what you need, want, and expect.

If you are lonely and you want somebody to listen, tell a woman. Most women are eager to please (so are most men), and if you tell a woman you are in the mood to talk, you will find she is more attentive.

If you need money and want to borrow from a woman, come right out and ask her. Don't buy her a drink, a steak, or a motel room if your goal is cash. Your chances are better when you play it straight.

If you need the services of a decorator or caterer, ask a woman to recommend one. She will always know the best for the money.

Women are also helpful if you need shopping advice, recipes, diets, information about books, plays, or movies.

And women are particularly helpful when you need a friend.

NEVER UNDERESTIMATE...

If women are the sex of underachievers—and they are—this is partly the result of generations of being underestimated. Thirty years ago *Ladies' Home Journal* coined the slogan "Never Underestimate the Power of a Woman." But that was an invention of the advertising promotion department and was designed primarily to boast of the power of a woman to buy an advertised product. The slogan became famous because it was used with a series of color cartoons which in themselves continued to underestimate the power of a woman.

Underestimating was the force that traditionally split the best dinner parties after the last course into two rooms of conversation. It wasn't that cigars and brandy could be enjoyed only in segregation. It was that the conversation that went with them—politics and business—was somehow just beyond the grasp of the females.

It was underestimating carried to the ridiculous that produced the strongly held belief that a male tennis player of any age and ability could best the world's number one female.

Perhaps it was underestimating that landed a

male collie the television role of Lassie.

More subtle and insidious is the underestimating we see daily in magazine articles supposedly addressed to women on so-called serious subjects. We remember one such series entitled "A Woman's Guide to . . ." Economics, balance of payments, computers, etc. The implicit suggestion was that the subjects would be explained primer-like so that even the female mind could absorb them.

Madame Curie, where are you?

NICE WOMEN

ice women, unlike nice guys, do not finish last.

That is because nice women are always there first, doing for others, thinking of others, helping wherever they can.

Nice women can be pretty (which makes the people who work for them think they can't be nice, too). And nice women do not give anyone unnecessary grief.

Nice women get more done in business than anyone else because they have innate taste, breeding, and manners. And nice women learn a very valuable lesson in business: people will do practically anything for someone nice. Even if the someone nice is a man.

NUDITY

ost women can survive—and some even thrive—on the freedom that accompanies nudity at home. The woman who accepts her body with little self-consciousness offers it the same way.

What is difficult for some women is group nudity: for example, the sauna with ten or twelve men and women. So if she is amenable to nudity en masse—and you can handle the idea, too—go ahead.

Otherwise keep your nudity, like your sex, a very private matter.

NURSES

With the exception of stewardesses, no group of women is more maligned than female nurses.

All a nurse really wants is to be treated with the courtesy due her profession.

If you are a patient, cooperate with the nurses who tend you.

If you are a relative of a patient, be courteous to nurses, and the patient you care about will get even more attention. Remember that the time non-patients take to chastise nurses is time nurses cannot spend with the patient you care about. Do not make unreasonable demands on nurses. Do not treat a nurse like a servant. And never ask to have regulations disregarded in order to accommodate you. Be certain to pay special-duty nurses on time, and cancel special nurses ahead of time.

If you are a doctor, never, never tell a single nurse you are not married if, in fact, you are.

Next patient.

ON THE ROAD

You just got the call. They want you to go to Another City for three days. You don't want to be away from her, so you ask. Yes, she's free, and she'll travel with you on your business trip. Before you leave, however, you ought to get a few things straight in this who-pays-for-what world. Incidentally, the same rules apply when you accompany her on a business trip.

1. Tickets. She pays for her tickets (when it is her expense account, you pay your fare).
2. Hotel registration. Long after mothers, spinster aunts, and possessive fathers accept the fact that unmarried people do live together, there will still be one small group that refuses to believe cohabitation exists. This group is known as the Room Clerks of the World. Room clerks are the ones who read your name upside down as you sign the hotel register. Room clerks are the ones who raise one eyebrow if you do not register as Mr. and Mrs. William Smith. So even though the mailman

knows you as Smith/Jones in 3D, the room clerk insists you be Mr. and Mrs. William Smith. If you are traveling on her expense account, registration becomes more complicated because you will have to be the nonexistent William Jones so that the room is in her name.

3. Hotel bills. You pay if it's your business trip. If it's hers, she does. On the other hand, neither of you charges drugstore purchases, barber, beauty shop, or other miscellany to the room.

4. Restaurants. When you entertain for the company and she is acting as your hostess, you pay for her—and vice versa.

OPEN-DOOR POLICY

emember when you used to get points for opening car doors, lighting cigarettes, and offering a tuck under the arm to ladies crossing streets?

Well, you can still do all those things and

remain as committed to equality as the woman to whom you extend the courtesies. Because that is what all of this is: a collection of courtesies. Good manners did not go flying out the window the day women received equal pay.

Consideration for a fellow human has nothing to do with his or her sex and everything to do with his ability to help himself.

It is still good manners to give up a seat to an older person (and that includes men). It is still gracious to rise when acknowledging an introduction to either a man or a woman. And it is stupid to run around a desk to seat a female who is obviously capable of seating herself.

Good manners should not get in the way of good business.

And vice versa.

OPEN MARRIAGE

Nena and George O'Neill popularized open marriage when they used those words for the title of their book several years ago. But did the O'Neills really mean sexual infidelity was terrific? It all depended on which TV talk show you saw them—because the book really gave you a choice.

What *Open Marriage* did say, openly, was that life improved considerably when both men and women permitted their spouses to attend everything from concerts to encounter sessions without each other.

No one can argue with this.

If you want to be successful with a woman, let her be herself, and she will be a lot more grateful than if you try to mold her like Silly Putty.

But if you really want to be successful with your woman, you will not only let her do those things that matter to her, but you will help her to reach her goals. And in a loving relationship she will help you.

Does she need money for the course she wants to take?

You can give it to her.

Do you want to invite four men to watch Monday night football in the den?

She can make sandwiches appear and children disappear.

Open marriage—open anything—is more than tacit approval.

It is physical, moral, and financial support.

It is open understanding.

OVER FORTY

**T**here once was a television commercial that showed all the different uses one could find for a coffee can. Well, that is the way it is with forty-year-old women these days. People are trying to find all different kinds of uses for them.

The best thing to do with a woman over forty is to treat her exactly as you did before she was forty.

The second best thing is to help her on with her life. Women who are over forty know it is never too late to study for a new career, to begin a new way of life, to move, to change in many ways.

For many women forty is no more fearsome than twenty-one or seventy, and once we learn that youth alone is not a reason for loving someone, we won't be afraid of age either.

PACKING BAGS AND OTHER DUTIES OF BUTLERS, FOOTMEN, ETC.

Packing bags is as personal a chore as cleaning drawers. And no woman should be expected to do either for a man.

Nor should a woman be expected to write his thank-you notes, extend his invitations, clean up after his poker parties, or buy his shaving cream.

Unless, of course, he is willing and able to do all the same things for her.

PATIENCE

exism and chauvinism have a long history, and a sketch of this history may help all of us appreciate the wisdom of patience in dealing with such deep-seated prejudices.

Certainly some of the blame can be laid on the attitude-makers of our Western civilization. The ancient Hebrew morning prayer had the men recite, "Blessed be God . . . that He did not make me a woman . . ." while the wives appropriately prayed, "Blessed be the Lord, who created me according to His will."

Among the Greeks, Plato thanked the gods, first for the fact that he had been created free instead of a slave, and secondly that he was created male instead of female.

Not that Christianity got off to any great running start. The Apostle Paul was just as bluntly disdainful of the comparative significance of women. He wrote in his letter to the Corinthians, ". . . forasmuch as [the man] is the image and glory of God; but the woman is the glory of the man. For the man is not of the woman, but the woman of the man. Neither was the man created for the woman, but the woman for the man."

Maybe King James needed his consciousness raised.

136

PAY

There still are men whose idea of equal pay is to pay according to need. Generally this means men are paid more than women because everyone "knows" that men have families to support and women can get by for less because theirs is a second income. Such paternalistic employers—until recently—were not sued, slapped, or censured.

But this is a new time, and the generations of male-female wisdom are more attitudinal than biological. In attitudes a generation is only five years, not thirty.

If you're authorized to offer a range of pay for the position, pay a woman the top figure. It means you expect more from her, and you will get it.

The law is very firm, very specific, and very rough on those who exploit.

PAYING THE CHECK

One of the sillier awkwardnesses that comes about in doing business with women is that men still feel compelled to grab for the check.

If a woman invites a man to lunch, she is going to feel put down if she isn't allowed the privilege of the transaction. Not that he will get much help from waiters, who still seem to panic when a man hands the check across to his hostess.

Maybe they are afraid that she can't compute the 15 percent for the tip. Or maybe they are afraid she *can* and would rather take their chances with the male for an overpayment.

One businesswoman who does a lot of entertaining made arrangements with her favorite restaurant not to present any bill at all, but to mail it to her. This saved embarrassment for waiter, guest, and hostess alike. But the right attitude on your part can make the whole arrangement unnecessary.

Chances are, when a woman invites you to lunch she is only looking for your business, not your body. Her virtue can remain as intact as yours for the price of a luncheon.

138

PERFECT WIFE

 bit of spoof, perhaps, but here for your sobering consideration is the following classified ad, purported to have been published in the London *Times,* January 15, 1817.

> FOR SALE, PERFECT WIFE. Speaks 3 languages—but only when spoken to. Expects nothing, and I have given her exactly that for 7 infinitely glorious wedded years—except for a hand-picked bouquet of violets every 9 months when she has another baby. Exceptionally skilled in woman's work. Stands just tall enough as to avoid looking awkward swinging an axe while chopping wood. £4 9d. or best offer. First owner. Box 1817. Dartmoor, England.

PERSON

Do you know today's secret word? It is *person. The Reader's Digest* has long promised that it pays to increase your word power, and here is a powerful word that certainly will pay.

All the joking that has gone on about dropping the sexist designation from mailman, paperboy, Congressman, craftsman, etc., may be telling us something. Think *person.* Use it whenever you might have said "man." Write it. Say it. Think it.

When it comes naturally to you, you'll be a better person.

POLITICAL WIVES

Political wives come in two varieties: those who want to be extensions of their husbands and those who do not. In dealing with a political wife and knowing that she almost always takes a back seat to her husband, you score well immediately if you congratulate her on *her* role. If she is his third arm, she'll be glad you noticed, and if she is her own woman, she'll be even more pleased.

Most political wives are shunted to the background. No one asks their opinion; they are bodies to be shipped to various groundbreakings, supermarket openings, and ox roasts where they smile, wave, shake hands, and tell what their husbands eat for breakfast. Political wives endure creamed chicken luncheons and hand-pumping constituents while their husbands are surrounded by hordes of able, attractive, politically motivated women, many of whom may indeed have more than political motivations.

As Mary Lindsay said *after* her husband, John, was no longer mayor of New York, "As long as there's a crowd . . . I don't mind. But if it's only one [woman], watch out."

POOLSIDE, OR BY THE SEA

Beware of strange women in bikinis. They often have strange men lurking in the background. Before you ask a woman you do not know what she is doing later, ask her the name of the book she is reading or the drink she is drinking.

If you are with a woman you know, it's still right and proper—despite liberation—to extend all courtesies. Make sure she has a chaise or a towel to lie on. Rub her back with suntan lotion and ask her to do the same for you. Go into the water with her, or watch so you are sure she is all right. Caution her if you think she is getting too much sun. Help her up and down (chaises), in and out (water)—and side by side it will be a lovely day.

POWER

Power, like a daisy chain, has historically linked men to men as they move horizontally to form coalitions that run industries, cities, counties, and countries.

Now that women are achieving power, however, they find no females who can give them the support real leadership requires. What is needed is a network of women who can communicate at top level and state the position of women in power in regard to social and economic issues.

Probably the most important things women in power can do are (1) to groom their successors, and (2) to recommend competent women to companies in which their talents can be used.

Another responsibility of women in power is to be certain that there is no sexual discrimination in regard to salary in middle management positions. Another responsibility is to make men aware that they cannot defuse power jobs and then make them available to women. An example was cited by Muriel Siebert, the first woman elected to a seat on the New York Stock Exchange and a woman considered for Treasurer of the United States. When she was

believed to be a candidate for the job, Muriel
Siebert had her attorneys do some investigating.
They found that the job had been stripped so
that it contained few responsible duties.

PREGNANCY

Yes, there are
some differences in women employees. They get
pregnant, for one thing.

You'll never have a better chance to show an
employee just how much you value her.
Experience and the law notwithstanding, there
still are too many organizations that seem to feel
corporately awkward about the blessed event
and have the policy "Get her out of here before
she shows."

Medical opinions and corporate opinions vary
widely, but the maternity-leave policy that
makes the most sense is one that permits the
individual to make her own decisions. In other
words, let her stay just as long as she really feels
like working, even up to a week away from
B-Day. If it doesn't work a hardship on the
expectant mother, it's hard to see how the rest of

the employees are disadvantaged. Certainly nothing else matters.

Whatever the policy, take the time to talk with the employee just as soon as you find out about her pregnancy. Let her know you want her back. Let her know that you think she will be even more valuable to the company when she returns, that her experience will be a benefit to all.

If it's her first baby, you should freely discuss any doubts she may have as to whether she will want to return to work right away. If she does return, try to establish some flexibility in work requirements that will permit her to feel she is not shirking any of the duties of her important new role. As for pay policy fair to both employer and employee, we recommend half salary up to six weeks and additional leave without compensation but with job guarantee for six months.

Finally, think again about whether your company is doing enough to help all young mothers to be happy both at work and at home. Good child care is good grown-up business.

PRESENTS YOU CAN LIVE WITHOUT

There is no feeling worse than that of opening a Christmas or birthday gift and discovering something you hate from somebody you love. And when your beloved stands at your side and murmurs, "Do you like it? Do you really like it?" what is a man to do?

Well, there are two things he can do. He can keep it or he can return it.

If she crawled through Arab bazaars to buy a flowered tie, you cannot very well return the treasure. But if it came from Saks or Gucci, you ought to be able to explain that you would like to go with her to make another selection.

The key is that you never return anything. You just go to the store with her and make another selection. The one she bought is too small, too big, or exactly like the one you already have and love.

In rejecting a present do not disparage her taste or question her sanity. Do not ask too many questions about her values . . . or she will begin to wonder why she ever got this far with you.

PRETENSE

en do a lot of dumb things where women are concerned, and one of the dumbest is in the name of kindness. In order to leave a wife, some husbands pretend outlandish untruths that result in unnecessary cruelty to their wives.

One husband pretended his wife could not satisfy him sexually. How could she when he was deeply involved with another woman? In an attempt to help his wife's sexual dysfunction the couple visited a marriage clinic. Now, after months of unsuccessful counseling, the distraught wife believes she is beyond help. She has yet to hear about the girl friend her husband has had for six years.

Another husband pretended to suffer from mental illness. Still another claimed to have lost his money and his job.

What husbands, lovers, and all men should understand is that truth is not only stranger than fiction, it is a lot easier to live with.

PROMISES, PROMISES

here are men who think they can make all sorts of fancy promises and win undying love.

Promise her marriage, and she will put her life on hold and wait until you feel ready.

Promise her a raise, and she will faithfully circle at fifteen thou over your desk.

Promise her a dishwasher, and she will make beef stroganoff.

Promise her a vacation, and she will work Saturdays.

Promises are terrific. They are hope in a handbag, the future carved in ivory. But there is something even better than a promise. It is called action.

Just remember that promises cannot be open-ended. And a promise is only as good as your follow-through.

QUIET, PLEASE

In this shoot-shoot bang-bang world there are few quiet times. So if the woman in your life doesn't want to hear you—or even John Chancellor—talk, maybe she has the right idea.

Somewhere in the noise and confusion of the world there must be times and places where we can be alone with our own thoughts. If the woman you love seems not to need you, remember that the time you give her alone will often improve the time you are together. Women who feel harried and do not take time to think for themselves seldom make effective and loving partners.

And you know something? You need time to yourself, too. A clinging woman is an annoyance to a man, and if the woman you care about seems to think that caring depends on how often you punch her personal time clock, remind her that you are still someone who needs his private moments. The community of minds is wonderful to behold, but sometimes the community of mind is more rewarding.

RAPE

O f all the calamities that can befall a woman, rape is still one of the most damaging to her psyche. This is due partly to the physical horror as the victim perceives rape and partly to the way the community perceives it.

There is still a body of elbow-nudgers who say knowingly, "She brought it on herself," but rape is not a tea party. And there are a lot better ways to get affection, attention, and interest.

Laws in these United States are not standardized, but some bills should be adopted by all state legislatures in order to make it easier to apprehend and convict rapists. And, in addition, we need:

1. A special state police "woman's desk" with a toll-free statewide telephone service that can be dialed any time of the day or night. A woman officer would take all information, follow up immediately with the proper local authorities. Too many local police officers dismiss rape reports as "exaggerations" or "woman problems."

2. A change in the rules of evidence in

rape cases so that the woman plaintiff
cannot be asked about her past sex life
on the witness stand.

The first of these two reforms would make it
possible for more women to report rape cases,
and the second would mean that more women
would be willing to prosecute suspected rapists.

READING

This little book is
designed to break the egg. You'll need a lot of
practice and more instruction before you
produce a soufflé. Awash as we are with
literature about the women's movement, the
following beginner's book list is offered for your
guidance:

**Born Female: The High Cost of Keeping Women
Down,** by Caroline Bird. New York: McKay
Pocket Books.
The Second Sex, by Simone De Beauvoir. New
York: Knopf, Bantam Books.
The Feminine Mystique, by Betty Friedan. New
York: Norton, Dell.

The Female Eunuch, by Germaine Greer. New York: McGraw-Hill, Bantam.

Sexual Politics, by Kate Millett. New York: Doubleday, Avon.

On Liberty, Representative Government, the Subjection of Women, by John Stuart Mill. London and New York: Oxford University Press. (Written in 1869.)

Feminism, edited by Miriam Schneir. New York: Random House, Vintage.

Our Bodies, Ourselves: A Book by and for Women, by the Boston Women's Health Book Collective. New York: Simon and Schuster, Touchstone-Clarion.

Between Myth and Morning: Women Awakening, by Elizabeth Janeway. New York: William Morrow and Company, Morrow Paperback Editions.

Masculine/Feminine: Readings in Sexual Mythology and the Liberation of Women, edited by Betty Roszak and Theodore Roszak. New York: Harper and Row.

RELATIONSHIPS

In all the talk about liberation, in all the conversation about the new woman, it still boils down to what men and women have always needed and always wanted from one another: a good relationship.

Relationship now, however, has a meaning that it never had. Relationship is more than a pretty word. Today relationship means the mutual workings of two people. Society no longer expects her to go 97 percent of the way. What is more significant is that she no longer expects to go 97 percent of the way. More and more people are understanding that sometimes the man goes further than the woman in making a relationship work, and sometimes the woman extends herself. But no one expects these extensions to be permanent. Instead there is awareness that relationships, like the ocean, are never the same. They wax, they wane, they intensify, and like the tide, they ebb.

Relationships do not just happen. They must be made to happen. In a love relationship we expect a certain chemistry to operate between people, but sometimes we forget that chemistry is a factor, too, between employer and employee, buyer and seller, parent and child. In all relationships it is important to understand what you cannot tolerate (the way she says hello, the nervous habits) so that you do not criticize another person for reasons that have nothing to do with your professed annoyance.

No relationship is easy, but courtesy and patience go a long way toward human understanding. And what is life without that?

REPAIRMEN

or most women, the only thing worse than having something broken is the experience of having someone fix it. Finding a repairman these days is trouble enough (and finding a repairperson is impossible). But then when he shows up, all too often it is with the suggestion, "This repair is really too complex to try to explain to a woman. Is your husband here?"

Just remember, you are working for *her*. She

found you, she hired you, she will pay you, and she will judge the results of your work.

If you want to talk to the boss on the job, you're looking at her.

RESTAURANT ETIQUETTE WHEN THE WOMAN PAYS

ell, here you are, knee to knee on a cozy banquette. You are her guest, and you both know it. You are about to hail the captain and order a drink for her . . . but you just remembered. She invited you. So what do you do?

If the captain is closer to you, let him know you're waiting. But don't be upset if she hails the captain. It's done everywhere now from Le Bistro to The Four Seasons.

When your order is to be given, it is correct for her as hostess to wait for you to make your decision.

She also orders the wine unless, of course, she asks your advice or preference. And when the wine comes to the table, she is the one who tastes it and decides whether it is worth your attention.

Don't expect her to help you with your coat, however. And do rise when she comes to the table. Remember she's still a woman . . . albeit a paying one.

RICH WOMEN

he only difference between rich women and rich men is the size of the holdings.

If you do business with a rich woman, you can expect her to be imperious, insufferable, and slightly suspicious of you.

If you love a rich woman, you can expect her to be confident, assured, and slightly suspicious of you.

Women with money, like their male counterparts, are never sure whether love and respect are tendered because of interest in them or their money.

The best way to get along with a rich woman is to allay her suspicions. In business you have to let her know that you can get along without her. She must not feel that she is responsible for your advancement or success because she will then be contemptuous of you.

If you really are in love with a rich woman, she must know that you do not need her money in order to live the life you are now living. She has to believe that you are willing to protect her, just as she knows she is able to protect you. And any time you can make a rich woman believe that you also think of her as an appealing woman, a womanly woman, she's on your side.

ROLE PLAYING

The time you have with your daughters stretches from the moment your nose is pressed against the glass in the maternity ward until your nose is pressed against the window watching a boy bring her home from that traumatic (for you) first big date. That isn't much time for the work at hand.

The responsibility you *must* share—even the

lion's share—is to prepare her to be tomorrow's woman. Little girls are not made only of sugar and spice and everything nice. Don't place that kind of burden on your daughter without allowing her a measure of puppy dog tails.

First, prepare her by example. The example of yourself at home. When your daughter sees you sharing the apron as well as the crown, she can begin to identify with you. Seeing that what *she* does at home *you* can do leads her to the exciting discovery that what you do at the office she can do as well.

Also, prepare her by suggestion. Ask your daughter what she wants to be when she grows up, with just as much seriousness as you ask your son. Ask, discuss, and ask again. Stretch her thinking now, and her ideas will never snap back to the old dimension. If she says she wants to be a housewife like Mommy, that's worth high praise from you. But then the question is, what *else* does she want to add to that career?

Finally, prepare her by surprise. Next Christmas, give *him* the toy working oven, and give *her* the model airplane kit. Santa's crazy, like a vixen.

Remember the password: Father knows best.

RUTS

There is nothing more comfortable than a rut. And most of us spend our lives in somewhat gilded ruts. Our ruts are comfortable because we retrace the ideas that give us comfort, repeat our political philosophies in rooms that do not change, and tell our secrets to people who have already heard them.

Yet there can be no growth, no expansion, no increase in our abilities if we do not get out of the ruts that have us mired in dreary sexism, phony liberalism, and unreal security.

All of us have to open ourselves to experience, make ourselves responsive to life. We have to read things we do not want to read, listen to people who say the things we do not want to hear, and so reroute our lives that we do not keep stopping at the same Hilton Hotels.

The best way to get out of a rut is to become better acquainted with ourselves. Take more time to make ourselves grow by reading, thinking, doing what we feel instead of what we "must."

Just once see if you can say, "To hell with business," and take a long walk by yourself.

SAY IT
WITH A NOTE

The greeting card business was invented by a man, for men. You can walk into a card shop now and go directly to a printed missive that supposedly phrases exactly what is in your heart—sympathy, affection, reward, a proposal, even a proposition. Though Cyrano de Bergerac might thumb his nose at the verse, you can lay down fifty cents and let the mailman deliver your fervent message encapsulated in rhyme.

But with women, true success comes with notes in your own words. You can let your fingers do the walking, but don't let Hallmark do your talking.

As the song says, just drop a line to say you're feeling fine. And you really will.

SECRETARIES

She is the daytime wife, the confidante, the one who knows as much about the business as he—and probably the most poorly paid person in the entire office.

Traditionally, secretaries have been live-in maids at the office, and some office manuals still contain coffee-making instructions for secretaries plus information on how to dust a desk top.

Those are the reasons intelligent, capable young women and men look with horror on job openings for secretaries. Yet a boss who understands that the job of secretary can be the training ground for future management personnel can recast the job and find good people. In hiring and working with secretaries today, remember:

- You can hire a male as well as a female.
- A good telephone personality is important (probably), and you had better determine the other needs of the job, such as typing ability.
- Don't ever ask your secretary to do messenger services.
- Do not berate a secretary in front of

others if you expect that person to stay with you and remain loyal.

- Help your secretary advance in your company.

SELLING YOUR PRODUCT (GETTING HER ATTENTION)

Last year when hairdressers told American women that they would instantly cut their hair and wear it short and frizzy instead of long and straight, American women just yawned and went on wearing their hair long and straight. They did not listen to hairdressers any more than they had listened to designers who four years earlier had told them to throw out their wardrobes and buy maxi dresses. Yet it is an older story than that. It goes back to the 1960s, when "doing your own thing" became the raging cry, and both men and women decided nobody was going to dictate fashion. Or much of anything else.

What this means to everyone who sells to women is that one no longer deals with a sheeplike attitude. Women are individuals, and you cannot put two consumers in one mold any more than you can two wives. You cannot generalize.

For that reason it is not easy to buy a woman's loyalty in the marketplace, because causes for loyalty vary. But despite the varying attitudes of women, they will respond if you sell *with* them, not *at* them.

If you act like the only man in the world, you will turn her off.

Inflation, world tension, to say nothing of individual health and family problems, are all competing for her attention. Women today do not have an easy time. They put up with small houses and cramped quarters, husbands who work too hard and husbands who do not work at all. In addition, women are readjusting their sexual and social roles.

In order to sell a woman, the first thing you have to do is make sure she knows you understand her. You have to find the way to tell her you know it's tough to be her. You have to be down-to-earth, talk on a one-to-one basis, and make her realize you are aware and sympathetic.

Selling a product is a little like selling yourself.

You do a lot better when you talk about her.

Or let her know you are listening.

SELLING YOUR PRODUCT (THE ADVERTISING)

irst, take the dish towel out of her hand.

You do not have to replace it with an atomic reactor, but you do have to stop acting as if the whole world were made up of housewives.

And in advertising you have to stop using the Housewife Mentality, which says to advertisers that if she is a woman she automatically cares only about her clean wash, her clean children, and her clean husband (generally in that order). Honestly, there really are other things that women care about.

These are some of them, goals which products and services can help her attain:

1. A feeling of well-being (as opposed to gorgeous, beautiful, or drop-dead sexy).
2. The sense of doing a job well (she doesn't have to overclean to be good).
3. A feeling of usefulness (you don't have to promise her the Carnegie Medal, but small heroism has its place in life).

4. Pride in her accomplishment (this can involve anything from saving money to increasing her knowledge).

Your advertising has a fine chance of succeeding if it doesn't make a woman feel like an electric broom, but instead makes her feel that by using your services she will understand and fill her life role better.

SELLING YOUR PRODUCT (THE CONSUMER ADVOCATE)

Advertising, also known as The Promise Business, has in recent years been responsible for promises that are more talk than truth, more sizzle than steak. In the wake of these business excesses we have had consumer excesses. Certainly the contributions made by Ralph Nader and other consumer advocates have caused business to police itself more carefully. On the other hand, honest companies are spending too much time answering letters, filling out questionnaires, and responding to governmental questioning.

As an advertiser there are some things you can do to lessen consumer pressure:

1. List all product ingredients on the package, even if the government does not yet require that this be done.
2. Stop making packages that belie the contents (the six-ounce package of Company A that is bigger than the eight-ounce package of Company B).
3. Make the information on package weight readable.
4. Don't keep introducing "me-too" products.
5. Instead of inventing needs, begin answering needs.
6. Don't overstate your ad claims for the product.
7. Don't promise services you cannot deliver.
8. Try to create an atmosphere of understanding if you are in the service business, and try to create an awareness of your industry if you sell a product.

Oh yes, one thing more: whatever you make, make sure it's good.

Good products can do more to silence consumer advocates than anything else.

SELLING YOUR PRODUCT (THE PROPOSITION)

If you really understand what women are about, you are aware of a woman's need both to escape from the everyday and to reward herself for enduring it.

She is the natural enemy of the person who takes her money at the supermarket check-out counter. She also hates with equal passion the gas company, the electric company, and the man from the finance company. She thinks the whole world is conspiring to take her money (and well they may be). She wants someone to reward her for this penny-pinching that is supposed to result in a well-fed family that is well dressed and well housed.

Now this is where you step in.

What will really turn a woman on today in the marketplace is a product or a service that permits her to fantasize and at the same time reward herself without feeling guilty.

Because we live in a world of kidnappers and drug pushers and bombers and robbers and rapists and people who take your seat on the bus, everyone needs to escape once in a while. Products and services offer that opportunity. The best promise you can make a woman today is the promise that for a short time anyway you will permit her to fantasize and take herself out of the ugly world into some place she can create.

The combination of fantasy/reward is where the marketplace is today with women.

This means that in selling a woman you have to present a proposition that permits her to change some part of her life without radically changing the way she and those who matter to her regard her and her role in society.

The promise cannot be too big, too overbearing, because your consumer is no fool. She is a woman who can be led gently into new areas of life. She is willing to experiment if you promise that she will not lose too much by testing and trying. She is willing to kick up her heels if you promise she will not simultaneously kick over the traces of her present life.

To sell a product, create a proposition that can challenge or comfort a woman or otherwise alter the way she feels about herself, and then support it with reasons.

The supportive reasons are the backbone of what we call the advertising.

SERVICE STATIONS

One of the few male domains left is the corner service station. There's something about the grease stains on the concrete, the wrenches on the wall, and the old tires piled up outside that seems to rule out women.

If success is your goal, and the service station is your game, forget about the men and welcome the women. Women are buying over half the gasoline sold in this country anyway, and they will respond a lot more loyally to any station that gives them service. Just like men, they are afraid of being sold parts and maintenance work they don't need, but they are also extremely nervous about damaging their cars through neglect. So if you are the kind of fellow who takes the time to explain the need for the new filter as well as the oil change, the business is yours.

Besides, what goes on under the hood of that modern monster has long since left the male just as ignorant as the female. Don't be condescending. Don't be flirtatious. When you ask her if she wants her oil checked, be sure you mean exactly that.

SEX

Don't.

Don't use it to get a raise, hold a job, or sell a carload of tractors.

Sex is a good, natural, warm thing between a man and a woman. It should be given out of love, accepted in the same spirit, and enjoyed in complete trust.

Sex isn't payment for your name, your friendship, or two tickets to the opera. Sex is not a weapon. It is not a way to open a deal or close a negotiation. If your number one weapon is sex, you obviously don't have much faith in your business abilities.

When the woman is the one who makes sexual promises, stand back and look again. You should never let a woman withhold sex as punishment. If she does, drop her. She's not worth knowing, sexually or otherwise.

Besides, women who flaunt sex usually have less of it than those who are buttoned up to the chin.

SEX APPEAL

In this day of accomplished women there are still men who cannot see beyond a thirty-eight-inch bust. Part of understanding the new woman is understanding the new sex appeal, for today sex appeal does more than meet the eye. Here are the new appeals that add up to sex appeal:

1. Job appeal. Everybody knows about the man who outgrows his wife, Poor Thing, and marries his secretary or her best friend. Now there is a new kind of job appeal: the attraction of equals. Brenda is the kind of woman who wouldn't get a second martini at a singles bar, but she is a shrewd and skillful media buyer. Once men get to know her in business they are so intrigued by her mind that everything, including her too-plump body, seems a lot better.

2. Talent appeal. Movie stars used to be the only ones admired from afar. But as women get more publicity for accomplishments that range from one-woman shows to political machinations, men are pre-sold on a

public image. For some men there is sexuality in a talented woman.

The most important thing to remember is that sex appeal, whatever its origin, is only the first step, and it is a clue that there may be something even better. It is the something even better that takes effort and skill to create.

SEX, OFFICE

ovies like *How to Succeed...* and plays like *Promises, Promises* have led us to believe that most office life today includes a lot of sexual foreplay, byplay, and aprèsplay. The lasses who serve Walter Matthau, we know, will be expected to give to more than the United Fund. Jack Lemmon, we assume, will be accosted at the water cooler by one who takes letters by day and gives it back at night. But that is fiction. In fact, life at the office may be every bit as fulfilling.

Most of the denials come from the bosses, but the boss is simply the last one to know. Some office people still think that the term "matinee" refers to an afternoon movie.

Management is always advising itself to stay away from the help: Don't seek favors at the office. But surveys show that when an executive does get involved, it is likely to be with someone on his own intercom. Most men, like most women, don't sit around thinking about the best hunting ground for a liaison. Dallying is something that just happens, and opportunity is often the major requirement. That opportunity usually comes with some break in the routine. The dinner break as a reward for working late. The much-maligned office party. Or, worst of all, the out-of-town business meeting.

The new liberation is a reminder that for men, as well as women, saying no never went out of style.

SHARING

Sharing is more than dividing the pie, splitting the income, and deciding who drives in the car pool. It is also accepting responsibility for the life of another person.

That acceptance of responsibility has to be communicated, and in the life of Susan

Marchand it was. As the president of Irvinware, a manufacturing company in New York, Susan Marchand went to Europe on a buying trip. Her husband decided to join her for a few days of skiing in Switzerland.

The first day he awakened with a cold and encouraged her to go alone to her ski lesson. When she returned to their room for luncheon, he said, "I watched you walk down the road this morning and I thought . . . what if something happens to her? She probably doesn't have any identification. So I wrote this on an envelope. Carry it with you."

She unfolded the envelope and there, in his handwriting, she read: "My name is Susan Marchand. If I have an accident, please notify my husband, Bob Marchand, at the Palace Hotel. He will take care of everything. He loves me very much."

The funny little envelope now is framed and sits on Susan's desk, a constant reminder that someone shares the responsibility in the living of her life.

SHOPPING

Sooner or later it had to happen. She had to ask if you would go shopping with her. She is going to buy a dress to wear to dinner with your best client (not hers), so how can you refuse?

Once you agree to shop with her there are certain courtesies:

1. If you do not like a dress she is trying on, tell her so. But you do not necessarily have to tell her the reason if the reason is that the outfit makes her look fat, old, like her mother or yours.
2. If you don't know anything about fabric, don't do the thumb-and-forefinger fabric test with everything she tries on.
3. If the dress looks good—but is too low-cut or too snug or just too sexy for her good and yours—tell her it is more than you can handle. She will respect your feelings.
4. If she is paying for the dress, do not ask the price. Besides, if you are not accustomed to seeing the price of

women's clothes, the cost will shock you.

5. Once the decision is made and the dress purchased, remember to notice it when she wears it.

SICK LEAVE

e all know that women are absent from the job a lot more than men. Or do we?

Even though the Bureau of Labor Statistics still credits men with a fractional advantage in this department, give women equal responsibility, equal pay, and an equal shot at the important new jobs in your organization, and women won't get sick of their jobs any more than men do.

SINGLE PARENTS: THE NEW MARKET

According to the United States Census Bureau, nine million children under age eighteen are being raised by only one parent, and for more than eight million of those children the one parent is a mother. The needs of the single parent are greater than those of the family in which two parents function because the single parent needs products and services which promise (1) less guilt in filling the parental role; (2) more mutually satisfying shared time with a child; (3) more energy to cope with the life role; (4) the ability to solve housekeeping problems.

The biggest mistakes are made when the single parent market is treated exactly like the nuclear family because "nukes" and "oners" have about as much in common as a suburban matron and a college student.

The single parent group is particularly responsive to advertising appeal because so little communication in the mass market is directed to their needs. With this market, as with all markets, the best results come when the audience feels the advertiser is talking one-to-one and

177

understands that every family does not look like the families on television programs. We are not all parents chosen from Central Casting with freckle-faced kids—and not every home has its very own mommy and daddy.

SINGLES BARS

There was a time when you would not find church sopranos in singles bars, but since there is so little action in the choir loft these days, singles bars are now a better cross section of America.

Before you go into a singles bar, however, you ought to be familiar with the code of ethics.

Most people in singles bars expect to buy their own drinks. As a man drinking with a woman, you do not have to pick up her check.

You may, however, wish to buy the woman a drink, and that is permissible.

Buy her two drinks, however, and you and she both know that is the unwritten signal that she intends to leave with you.

Three drinks, and she may be your next roommate, so be careful.

Singles bars are not the new YMCA, and they do attract some people you might not find particularly desirable. So keep your eyes open, and if you are looking for a pleasant evening's entertainment, you just might find it at a singles bar. Then again, you might find more than you are looking for.

SKIING

The best advice we can give about skiing is, don't. If you persist, however, one way to get a return on your investment of physical risk is to make skiing part of your success program with women. She's a lot less likely to snap in two than you are, and you may need somebody to whistle for the Saint Bernard.

If you've been fooled by beer commercials and old movies of Sun Valley into thinking that this is a sexy and zestful sport, go to the bottom of the hill and start over. It's essentially cold and awkward and humiliating, but skiing with a woman companion does offer a certain bond of suffering not always available elsewhere. Some rules to schuss by:

1. Choose a companion of comparable skill and experience. Otherwise it will be a bore for one of you and a chore for the other.

2. Let her pay for her own tickets and rentals if she offers. Skiing is a sport of great independence (as well as horrendous expense), and she may well prefer to keep it that way.

3. If you've never skied together before, start by taking a group lesson with the instructor. One lesson isn't going to do much for your form, but you'll learn how difficult a slope to start on.

4. Help her on with her boots and her bindings because this can be a nail-breaking chore even with modern equipment. When you're moving onto the chair lift, give her the outside position. This indicates you may know a little more about what you're doing than you really do.

5. Don't push your luck. When you get tired or cold or nervous, which will probably be before she does, that's the time to quit. And after quitting is the only time to start the wine, no matter what the Europeans say.

SLEEPING

Not all time in bed with a woman is spent in sexual activity. Every once in a while you have to sleep. And sleepy-time etiquette is something that is seldom discussed.

If you sleep in a double bed, share the blankets. Don't tuck them all around you and expect her to figure out whether or not to wear her bunny slippers in order to avoid freezing.

Hold her—not because you are getting ready for the Big Move—but because you're not. Hold her close, make her feel loved, and then turn over and go to sleep.

If you can't sleep, don't turn and toss and keep her awake. Get out of bed, go to another room, and read, paint, brush your teeth, or write a letter to your mother.

Settle on a comfortable room temperature for the two of you. Don't—as one little boy once said—suffer-cate. On the other hand, it is not necessary that you qualify for the Polar Bear Club right there in your very own bedroom.

When the alarm goes off in the morning, turn it off, then reach for her, and start your day by letting her know with a touch, a sweet caress, that you still love her.

SOMEBODY ELSE'S CHILDREN

Sure you're crazy about her. But what about those tiny tots in her custody?

You may be able to handle a relationship with a woman who has been married before, but how do you handle your relationship with her children? It does require special and kindhearted attention. It also requires a more generous spirit. You may get annoyed with your own children, but then you're their father. It's difficult to reprimand someone else's babies, and you should not try.

It is important to remember that her children are competing with you for her attention, and they are probably going to resent your presence and their mother's obvious interest in you. Also they are wondering whether you are going to be the new daddy in their household.

If the children's father is living and is devoted to them, they will also resent you for his sake.

This doesn't mean you have to stop seeing the woman you care for. It just means that you have to care enough to watch the way you talk and act in her home . . . as compared to the way you would talk and act in your very own love nest.

STAY-HOME PAY

he old adage that reads "Equal pay for equal work" is accepted by the man on the street. Then why is it that we are willing to accept "no pay for equal work" for the homemaker?

What about the woman who through choice or necessity stays home every day to take care of a family and manage the increasingly big business of running a household? She still sees no money coming back to her in the form of a paycheck. Neither does she establish her true worth in terms of coin of the realm nor earn credit with Social Security so that she can look forward to retiring from her labors as a man does. She cannot even count on receiving Brownie points for her efforts from friends and family.

This is ridiculous. Any number of studies has been conducted to compute the market value of the services performed by the homemaker—scullery maid, chauffeur, bookkeeper, cook, gardener, mistress—and the latest average replacement cost for these efforts is $12,000 a year.

But is there a single housewife who receives a check for these services or receives due credit from her contemporaries for effort expended or success achieved?

Don't be the kind of man who has to pay for it to appreciate it.

STUDENTS

ho is doing well in graduate and professional schools?

You'll never guess.

According to Dr. Saul Feldman, author and teacher, divorced women are among the best and most dedicated of all students in the nation's colleges and universities.

And who are the least productive?

Married women.

Professor Feldman believes that the strain of marriage prevents women from achieving their highest potential.

Of course, the answer is not divorce. The answer is a redistribution of responsibility in the family and a better and more supportive role played by the husband.

Professor Feldman found that the pattern

184

reversed itself among men. Married men are very productive students.

How can we make married women more productive students?

Probably by giving them husbands who are supportive, and short of that, by changing attitudes in society.

SU CASA OR MI CASA

If she is spending the night at your house:

- Don't make any other telephone calls, particularly calls to other women.
- Don't recall all the times and all the women who have slept in her place in that very bed.
- Be sure you provide her with such essentials as makeup remover, toothbrush, and body lotion. (She may think such thoughtfulness is for her, but let's face it—it's really for you.)

- Close the door when you use the bathroom.
- Make sure your apartment is neat. Even if you are a bachelor, a sloppy pad can turn a woman off.
- While she undresses, let her know you're watching . . . a word or a gesture will do.
- In the morning you make the breakfast bacon, and then take her home, to her office, or escort her to a cab. No woman wants to leave his place without him.

If you are spending the night at her place:

- Offer to bring a bottle of wine, some cheese, records, or other inducements to lovemaking.
- Don't tell her what is wrong with her apartment. If she decorated it, she loves it.
- Offer to get up and get extra blankets. Even though it's her house you can extend some courtesies.
- Don't ask whether you are the first man she has brought home; she might tell you the truth, and you'd better be sure you can handle it.

SURPRISES

For most of us and for the most part, life is a series of repeat broadcasts. Tomorrow is no more likely to be different from today than was yesterday. The fact that life today was without tragedy is not quite enough, because chances are it was also without glory. The dailiness of life wears especially on women, who are more likely to feel trapped with repeated chores and predictable schedules.

This is where you come in.

Pleasant surprise is what the soul needs, and it takes such a little effort. Gifts at Christmas, for birthdays and anniversaries are invariably appreciated, but expected. A gift without occasion is one that thrills.

When was the last time you surprised your wife by keeping your calendar open and inviting her to lunch?

George Delacorte, a successful New Yorker who knows how to please women through the experience of his four-score-and, calls his wife from the office and takes off two hours to go with her on a shopping trip. Talk about a surprise!

So you don't have time? You have time to take

off to watch the World Series, don't you? Be the world champion yourself.

Or just pick up the telephone and call her. Not for an errand. Not for a reason. Just for the surprise.

SWEET TALK

If you think women working today are more attractive than they used to be, you're right. They both look and feel younger longer. It's because women are in business until retirement, not until procreation. And the woman who has added purpose and ambition to her character is one of enormously greater sexual attraction.

For this woman of today, "sweet talk" in the office is as out of date as Amos and Andy jokes. Straight talk has replaced syrupy paternalism and the condescending tone.

Remember, she is purposeful. She doesn't want superficial flattery; she'll work hard anyway. She is looking for honest praise from honest co-workers.

TAKING CARE OF A WOMAN

This means different things to different men. To a man who thinks she is his baby doll it can mean anything from buttering her toast to writing her checks. To a dyed-in-the-wool chauvinist it can mean a broad wink, a nudge in the ribs, and the words, "All she needs is a man to take care of her . . . if you know what I mean." To a man who is aware, taking care means being interested when asked, helpful when possible, understanding when necessary, and kind always.

So take care what you mean when you say "take care."

TENDERNESS

It is not true, it just is not true that tenderness is something God gave only to women. Men have it; it's just that they don't always get around to using it. They should, however, because . . .

It is not weak, it is not immature, it is not soft to be *solicitous* when anyone (woman or man or child) seems to need help.

It is not phony if you are *easily touched* and show your emotions, particularly at important times in your life (that includes recognizing and acknowledging recognition of love).

It is perfectly all right to be *affectionate* when you honestly feel affection—a hug, a small kiss, a quick embrace are simply ways of letting a woman who matters know that she does.

You will not lose your reputation for virility if you show *consideration*.

And you will probably enhance your reputation as a human being.

TENNIS

No other game played with racquets can be as much fun for mixing the sexes as tennis, now that Bobby Riggs has freed men from the slavery of having to win. Here are a few tips for having more tennis fun.

Don't assume that you're the better player when you team up for mixed doubles. Don't move automatically to the backhand court, but give your partner the choice of sides. Same for first serve.

Don't patronize. When she makes a bad shot, you both know it and words won't help.

Don't modify your serve for a woman unless she specifically requests that you do. Most women play for the challenge of the sport and do not want to be mollycoddled.

If you call foot faults for her male partner, call them for her. Again, she does not want special favors.

If it's just a tennis game and not a date, you can expect her to get to the court under her own steam, and it is not necessary that you arrange her transportation.

If you are playing at a court where it's possible for you to buy beverages after tennis, then make the offer. Equality does not mean less gentlemanliness (it means more).

If you are playing singles, offer to spot her the necessary games in order to make the set competitive.

If her game is better than yours, don't keep apologizing and wondering why you can't return a shot that would trouble Arthur Ashe.

Don't poach by moving into her territory to take the critical shots. If you do, you *deserve* to have your head split open with her steel racquet. Remember, this is not the time for instruction, so don't give advice unless she asks for it. Above all, never, never groan.

Oh yes, remember to bend your knees.

THE ABORTION

bortion isn't something that happens just to women. In every instance it happens to a man, too.

If you are the party of the second part, don't wait for an invitation. Step forward and volunteer. You did before, didn't you?

Abortion is a legally and medically accepted solution to a problem, so there's no need for you to go into hiding. Start out by making the arrangements at the hospital. Plan to pay the bill. And feel lucky if she will let you.

Abortion is something that happens to companies, too. If you're the boss, remember that an absence for this reason is simple medical leave, so don't treat it as more, corporately. But personally, treat it as more. She's not having a tooth pulled, you know.

Don't be backward. Be the kind of boss she can talk to. You aren't needed for a moral judgment, but you are needed to help ease the trauma.

THE MORNING AFTER

irst, no matter who you are, understand that sex within the organization chart—outside of marriage—is destructive. To you.

There is no way to keep the office love affair a secret. You don't tell anybody—except in confidence; she doesn't tell anybody—except in confidence; and everybody knows. Now you find out that all the world does not love a lover. Possibly there is envy, certainly there is resentment, and nobody can win.

Do you fire her? No. Does one of you get another job? Yes. Or simply agree to stop seeing each other, and surprise the world by living up to the agreement.

THE PACK MENTALITY

 all it camaraderie. Call it bull sessions. Call it a night out with the guys. No matter what you call it, it is still "Pack Mentality," that identification that some men get only when they are with groups of men.

The Pack Mentality causes normally responsible men to revert to boyish pranks. Its roots are probably in boyhood friendships that are best expressed through pushing, shoving, and tackling one another.

The Pack Mentality is not often dangerous,

and in many cases it is a healthy release for men who want to forget they are men every once in a while.

Where it offends women is when it is a hostile and clannish gathering, a sex binge, a heavy drinking or gambling time. Women do not expect to own men and their time, but also they do not expect men to turn against them in angry and vindictive ways when they are not there.

So before you pick up the Pack Mentality, better check the pack and see if it's your brand.

THINGS TO KNOW BEFORE YOU EVER TRY TO SELL A WOMAN ANYTHING

Generalizing is a dirty and dangerous trick, but there are some things about women that provide useful clues, so at the risk of letting you think all women are alike, here are a few ways that they are; ways to consider before you try to sell a woman anything.

1. Women are generally suspicious of contracts and other legal documents. Men are, too, but women are not afraid to say so.

2. All women have more money than you think they do. Women squirrel their money—under panty hose, in a jewelry box. She always has more cash than you thought she did.

3. When it comes to her appearance, her hair matters most. If her hair doesn't look the way she wants it to, she hates the way she looks, no matter how pretty her face or handsome her clothes.

4. Give her facts. She can and does read direction manuals, information sheets, and she resents half-truths and overly cute approaches to no-nonsense products and services.

5. Don't talk down to her. All her references are not in the area of home, motherhood, and frost-free refrigerators. She knows about détente, shortages, inflation . . . and frost-free refrigerators.

6. Get your foot in the door with an idea that helps her, not you. Sales approaches that begin with "new," "introducing," and "revolutionary" are just a big ho-hum to the buyer.

7. Most women are bored. If you can present a way of changing their lives without altering their self-image or the opinions of those who matter to them, you will win a woman.

THREATENING WOMEN

One of the main reasons both men and women oppose liberation is fear of the threatening woman. But are women really threatening men, or are they forcing men to regard themselves in new ways?

Most women do not deliberately threaten men or other women. So if you feel threatened, what do you do about it? How do you keep the new woman from becoming a threatening woman?

By increasing your talents and abilities. Why not go back to school if the woman in your office seems to know more about computers than you do? What's wrong with taking a course in the arts if it is going to make you converse more comfortably with someone else . . . and comfortable conversing is just another way of giving you more confidence.

Try ending your own feelings of possessiveness if you are threatened by your mate. Remember that your mate is not a threat if you regard her as her own person entitled to sole authorship of her opinions, ideas, and actions. She is not your chattel, and you are not responsible for each word she utters. She may split her income tax with you, but you don't own half her life. Relax and start to enjoy her for a change.

Define your own ambition. Are you eager to do good things for their own sake, or are you simply interested in doing better than someone else? Is your interest in what you have done, or is your concern about what you have not done?

In this society of winners and losers, what is it about women that is really threatening you?

Jealousy maybe? Or is it self-contempt?

TRAVELING SALESPERSONS

Sure, you know the one about the traveling salesman and the farmer's daughter, but do you know the one about the traveling salesperson and the men *she* meets?

Today, as women seek stronger management positions, they are learning that one route is through sales, and many major companies are making their sales forces co-ed.

Women are selling everything from

heavy-duty machinery to pharmaceuticals. They are more than cosmetics ladies or representatives for the telephone company. Some women are earning more than their husbands.

And this poses problems for the men who are the customers of the new salespersons. Do you offer them a cigar, a chair, or just an order?

Dealing with the salesperson is, as always, a matter of courtesies extended. She expects exactly what the man she replaced expects:

- She expects you to keep your appointments and not let her cool her heels in your waiting room while you make telephone calls you could make just as easily another time.
- She expects you to listen to her sales pitch and not interrupt with cute, sexist remarks about her big eyes or her big anything.
- She expects you to give her exactly the kind of order you would give her male counterpart.
- She expects to take the plant tour with you and not be excused because of her sex.
- She expects to take you to lunch if that's what you permit male salesmen to do.

Most of all, she expects to do so well that she won't be in sales forever.

TRAVELING TOGETHER (BUT NOT THROUGH LIFE)

In an inspired moment your boss decides that when you take the next trip to visit the secondary markets you also take the new third assistant in the marketing department. She happens to be a female. What do you do?

1. Assume she is a liberated woman, liberated enough so that she knows you are not responsible for her. Both of you are responsible to the company—period.

2. If you have friends in the city you are visiting and do not want to have dinner with your traveling companion, inform her in advance. Despite her new freedom, she still has a lot of old fears, and if you don't tell her in advance that you won't be inquiring about her dinner plans, she might feel that she did something wrong. And as everyone, male or female, knows, no one can

afford to have an ego damaged any more than is absolutely necessary.

3. Treat her exactly the way you do in the office. If she's your pal there, then she's your pal on the road. And if you want to keep the relationship a business one, then don't discuss your marital problems with her.

4. When you get home, don't tell your wife how smart, talented, informed, and attractive you found The Other Woman. If your wife has been spending the past two days hanging out the wash while you were hanging out in cute little Italian restaurants . . . oh well, you can figure it out.

TYPING

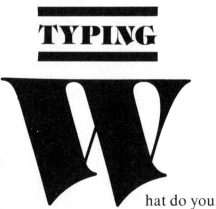

hat do you mean, God never intended you to be a typist? He gave you fingers, didn't He?

There is nothing that makes a woman feel

more subservient than typing résumés, letters,
and sales reports for the man she lives with. Even
if he hunts and pecks, she'll appreciate his
willingness to type it himself.

No woman wants to be an at-home secretary
any more than a man wants to be an after-hours
repairman.

UNDERSTANDING WOMEN

Hollis
Summers, a man who writes understandable
poetry, was approached by an intense young
woman after a reading. "Why," she asked, "are
women poets such as Sylvia Plath and Anne
Sexton suicide victims?" Hollis took one small
step back, looked carefully at the woman,
smiled, and said, "The answer is yes."

The point of that anecdote is that we really
don't have to understand women or men. We
have only to accept them in whatever flawed
form we find them and through acceptance give

each other some of the human comfort we all seek.

In other words, gentlemen, you don't always need an answer. There are still times when a shoulder will do.

VIOLENCE

Along with all the books on sadomasochism has sprung a new cult based on the belief that women thrive on violence. It isn't true.

Throw away the black whips and leather gloves. Women who feel good about themselves do not want beatings to know that you care. They are not looking for any other cruelties either.

The best way to ensure a long and loving relationship with a normal woman is still the normal route: gentleness.

VIRGINITY

To some the contemporary definition of virginity is "no intercourse until the third date." But if you are an old-fashioned man with respect for old-fashioned virtues, are you sure you are not putting sexual pressures on a woman? Are you absolutely certain that you are not encouraging her to be permissive while at the same time hoping she will not be?

Teasing is an old trick for both men and women, and it is shabby no matter who plays the game.

If you don't want her to go to bed with you, stop making her think she has to. And if you do want to go to bed with her, but want to wait, tell her. Honesty still does a lot more to advance and preserve a relationship than good acting.

WAITRESSES

Long ago someone got the idea that waitresses are Everyman's Sex Object. So waitresses generally have held their tempers while men held (or tried to hold) everything from the waitress's elbow to her ankles.

There is no reason to be more flirtatious with a waitress than you are with any other woman who casually appears in your life. If you really like a waitress, the best way to let her know is with a generous tip.

WEEKEND WONDERS

Y ou know them. They shoot the rapids, ride the trails, ski the big ones, swim the Channel, and throw the discus.

All on weekends, of course.

That would be all right if they didn't expect their women to keep up with them.

If you are an outdoorsman, good for you. But do not expect her to keep up with you when it's twenty degrees below zero. And don't expect her to go skinny-dipping in Lake Michigan in February.

Athletics are for athletes, and if the woman you're with is less than comfortable with heavy-duty sports, try something she can handle. Like toasting marshmallows in front of a roaring fire.

WHAT WOMEN NEED

Being truly successful in any relationship usually requires looking at the elephant through the other person's eyes. Sure, women's needs are human needs, but you may just have been through enough inhumanity to spoil your focus. Here are some of the needs of women today:

1. *To be an individual,* not a mass-produced consumer or statistic.
2. *To achieve full status as a person,* not solely as a wife or mother.
3. *To have attention.* From you. From her family and friends. From the community. From business. This need to communicate is what produces the epidemic of busy signals in the world's most sophisticated telephone system.
4. *To feel young.* (Thought you were the only one, didn't you?)
5. *To feel modern.* The shoe may not fit, but she's going to wear it anyway.
6. *To feel creative.* There may be numbers underneath the paint on the canvas, but the pride is pure Old Master.

7. *To be inspired, uplifted.* A little weekly newspaper named the *National Enquirer* sells 200 million copies a year. Almost all in the supermarket, and almost all to women. What is the secret of this phenomenon? Inspiring stories of common folk who, though living by the rules, have suffered extreme adversity and who, still living by the rules, have triumphed through perseverance and faith.

8. *To have a sense of purpose.* In the past it was hard to refute the biological evidence that the purpose of a woman's life was to bear young. Then came the Pill, with directions that guaranteed contraception. But the Pill didn't come with directions as to what new purpose would replace the old. That is the question. And that is what women and men need most—purpose.

WHISTLING

There is a strong belief among many women that being whistled at by construction workers, cabdrivers, and men on the street is demeaning.

But obviously both women and men are sex objects in certain circumstances, and if a man who sees a woman only once sees her as a sex object . . . so what?

It is the man who sees a woman frequently who must understand that she is more than a sex object.

In other words, it's okay to whistle on the street. But don't whistle while you work. At home you're on your own, depending on the way your mate views her sexuality.

WHO'S ON FIRST?

Everybody is supposed to be able to work and play and understand in just what proportions both give satisfaction. If you are the only one in your nuclear family or loving relationship or what-have-you who works, then it is not too difficult to decide whose career comes first and how much play you both need. When she works, it isn't quite so simple.

In order to support two careers there must be mutual agreement. There still are men who cannot handle the thought of a wife who earns more than a husband, but a man who gives a woman a sense of herself has not shortchanged his woman, no matter what each earns.

The manager of a supermarket in Chicago said, "My wife is getting her master's, so in a couple of years she will make more money than I do. But what's the difference? So she'll have a checking account, and I'll have a checking account. What the hell, no matter how much money she makes, I know this chick is nuts about me."

If you do love her, then you can understand her long hours . . . and not worry because the man at the desk next to her earns more than you do.

If you do love her, you don't have to be afraid she will leave you because she is ashamed of your job.

If you do love her, you will give the psychic and spiritual help she will need to overcome her own fears about her job and her abilities.

And if she loves you, she will understand that it is still impossible to combine a job outside the home with a smooth-running household unless there is a man liberated enough to let it happen.

WHY DO I LOVE YOU?

Is it the blue eyes or the green sweater?

Is it the soaring intellect or that she dusts like your mother?

Most of us do not really know why we love the people we do, but one woman was able to verbalize her feelings. She is a successful woman who has had her successes with men, too, and for years she has been faithful to just one man. Why?

"Because," she said, "he loves me. He loves me even though he has seen me at my worst, at times when I don't really deserve to be loved. He has loved me then. And he has loved me at good times, too." Then she paused and said, "I suppose that sounds very selfish."

What most of us fail to realize is that love is not all giving, and if we are honest with ourselves and those we love, we plan to take, too. We want to take. We need to take. And although we look for a lot of worldly reasons to love another, one of the strongest reasons for love is that we are loved.

Do you love somebody enough to be loved in return?

WIDOWS

A widow is not a half-person any more than any other unmarried person. Immediately following the loss of a husband, women are innundated with flowers, briskets, and donations to charities. What widows really need is less attention at the time of the funeral and more attention following it.

The best thing you can do for a widow is help her resume a normal if different life.

Can you help her get a job?

Move?

Take her children for an afternoon, evening, or special treat?

Invite her for Christmas, Thanksgiving, or New Year's Eve?

Introduce her to a new man?

If a woman who works for you is widowed, sit down and talk to her honestly. Give her a chance to vent her anger, grief, and frustration. Usually she cannot say what she feels to those who are also emotionally involved, but as someone deeply concerned with her welfare, you can give her the opportunity to talk unguardedly. And should you have a recent widow in your employ, don't be afraid to give her a new, challenging assignment. At the time of widowhood work can be a salvation.

WINE LISTS

Nobody should be intimidated by a sommelier, a wine list, or a haughty headwaiter.

As you undoubtedly know, it really does not matter whether you drink red or white wines with meat or fish. It matters only that you order what you want.

If the restaurant has a sommelier, let him make the wine choice for you.

When you are faced with a wine list and are unsure of the list and nervous about the price, ask the waiter to bring you a carafe of house wine. House wine is usually good, generally inexpensive, and when you order it you sound as if you know what you are doing.

WOMEN'S WORLD

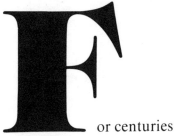

or centuries women's world was thought to be triangular: *Kinder, Kuchen, Kirche.* For some women it still is. But with the increased opportunities in women's work have come new attitudes:

1. *Housekeeping.* Cleanliness was next to Chipso at one time, but it's been a long time since we've seen any Chipso. The rewards of a spotless house are in serious question.

2. *Food preparation.* Slaving over a hot stove is for slaves, and it's hard to keep slaves around when there aren't any masters. Today's enlightened cook knows that a forty-five-minute meal that tastes good and contains the four essential foods for good nutrition beats a feast that takes four hours to prepare. Chopping and dicing and mincing refer to prizefighters.

3. *Fashion.* Fashion isn't dead. It's alive and well and living on the backs of the public rather than in the kinky minds of a few French designers. Increasingly

women are finding out that fashion means looking good and feeling right and requires only the sanction of their own mirrors.

4. *Leisure time.* Women never had any, so they know better than to expect any now. But there are hours filled with self-improvement courses, continuing education programs, and hobbies that are infinitely more self-expressive than the sonnets of yesteryear.

And when was the last time anybody darned your socks?

WOMEN IN TELEVISION

No television person is more visible than Barbara Walters, yet even the redoubtable Ms. Walters announced, when she served as anchor person on Election Night, that she was playing too important a role for women in TV. What Barbara deplored was the fact that she did not have the luxury to fail. If she did poorly, the networks could calmly say, "See—women are no good in that job," and if she did well, it wouldn't necessarily mean that every network would get its own woman to anchor the news or specials. As it happened, Newsperson Walters did well and has since become the first woman to anchor a television special.

Does this mean that women will move ahead fast?

Not necessarily.

Women are still stuck in weather-girl roles, and stations still clamor for black women ("You see, Bill, you get two minorities for the price of one"). But liberation does not occur every time a station manager puts a black woman in front of a camera.

Nor does liberation happen when women are hired as receptionists and typists. Television, the most influential of all media, holds an important key to understanding between men and women. What TV puts on the air is vital in furthering that understanding, but what TV does behind the scenes also influences program content.

Since television is a regulated industry and must be an equal opportunity employer, what is needed is a little more equality in terms of producers, directors, floor people. And a little more equality in the front office, too. Women station managers of America, stand up and be counted—both of you.

WORKING HOURS

If you are the boss around your shop, your real job is to do whatever you can to make it possible for the rest of the people to get their work done. Remember that when you set the office working hours. More than in any other phase of business, women need special consideration at the time clock. The working mothers—maybe your best performers—have special demands at home that may conflict with office work only in the matter of hours, not interest. Put in a test for flexible office hours, permitting employees to come in an hour early in order to leave at four o'clock. The rewards to a mother of being home when the kids burst in from school will only make the work they do for you that much better.

Remember when you threw open the door and shouted, "Hey, Mom, I'm home"? A lot of working mothers don't want to miss that greeting. Flexible hours may be a plus that makes working for you better than working for anybody else.

WORKING WIVES

ll working
wives are not brain surgeons or steeplejacks, but
even if they have less exotic jobs, they do have
one thing in common: they are damned tired by
nightfall. The idea of romance on the side is
laughable to the woman who can hardly turn on
her side by the time she crawls into bed after
eight hours on the job followed by home work:
cooking, cleaning, and speaking sternly (or
warmly) to the children.

Next to a good mattress the best thing you can
give your working wife is a helping hand. Pick
up a dish towel—and use it. Pick up your
socks—and wash them. Pick up the kids—and
deliver them to Cub Scouts, tap dancing,
encounter sessions, or whatever "growth
experience" their frenzied parents think they
need.

Decide who will pay which bills—and then
don't discuss money.

Open separate checking accounts—and don't
ask her about each check she writes.

Don't pry about her job—she'll tell you what
she wants to tell you.

Give her advice—but only if and when she
asks for it.

Respect her job and the way she regards it.

Don't make dates without checking them first with her.

Keep yourself interesting, alert, well-groomed. She sees a lot of appealing men all day, and if you are going to sit around in your jockey shorts watching Saturday basketball, Sunday hockey, and Monday night football, she just might get the idea that you are a man she is fast outgrowing.

WRITERS TO READ BY

If you think all women writers are still turning out *Pride and Prejudice*, watch your flanks. Some of them are using the words, describing all the acts you've heard about, and adding a few more that will leave you back at the old medical dictionary. And some have been writing since the early 1900's.

To see what's going on behind the little Olivettis, read Erica Jong, Lois Gould, Fay Weldon, Penelope Mortimer, Dee Wells, Doris Lessing, Paula Fox, Colette, Virginia Woolf,

Edna St. Vincent Millay, Jill Robinson, Joyce Carol Oates, Anne Roiphe, Adrienne Rich, Maxine Kumin, Nikki Giovanni, Gail Sheehy, Germaine Greer, Iris Owen, Rona Jaffe, Anais Nin, Anne Morrow Lindbergh, Dory Previn, Judith Viorst, Erma Bombeck, Maya Angelou, Lillian Hellman, Shana Alexander.

These will do for starters—now add your own favorites.

X-RATED MOVIES

You may not be the Porno King on your block, but let's face it. You do get your kicks (or at least some of them) looking at x-rated movies and magazines. So what do you do when you meet a woman who finds pornography a turn-off instead of a turn-on?

First, understand that not all women can accept pornography. Their mothers didn't like it, and their teachers told them it was wicked. If you like her, respect her feelings and don't make her think she is outdated, square, or saintlike if she says no to the green door.

Second, go without her. Go to the films you want to see. Buy the magazines you want to read. Your needs are not the same as hers, and there is no reason you have to stay home and watch kiddie cartoons, because she thinks you should. She had her chance to join you; she said no. Now act for yourself.

Thoughtfulness means not only thinking of others' needs and wants. It means thinking of yours.

YEARS AND YEARS AND YEARS... WITH THE SAME WOMAN

It is a funny thing, but when you promise to love, honor, and cherish, the years stretch before you like an inviting road. When you look back you are amazed at how tangled the path has become.

Marriage, at best, is not easy to make interesting. A woman who married her lover after a ten-year courtship said, "I think marriage is better for us. I know I would rather be married, but I have to admit I miss those romantic flights for secret weekends."

Romance, as they used to say in the magazines, does not have to end when marriage begins.

There are ways to keep love fresh. Assuming first that you do not bore each other, you can plan small adventures: dinner at a favorite restaurant when she doesn't expect to go out, two tickets for a trip she did not know about. And you can let her know that there is no reason she cannot do the same kind of thing for your relationship. Let her know you'd like it if she were to buy two tickets for the basketball game. And if you want her to do it again, make sure you show your appreciation. There is nothing more dispiriting than doing kind things for a man or woman who yawns and says, "What's next?"

ZIP (RHYMES WITH HIP)

 here is nothing like a man who's with it.

The most enchanting, engaging kind of man is the one who is aware of the world he lives in. He

223

is the politician who is not all politics. He is the businessman who is not all business. He is the entertainer who is not always on. There is a story about an actor who was dining with a beautiful young woman. All through dinner he told her about his career, his hit plays, his talent. Then when dessert arrived he said, "Ah, my dear. Enough about me. Now let's talk about you. What did you think of me in my last role?"

A one-track man will never get on the right track with a woman who matters to him.

Nothing is perfect. Especially life. But if you approach this funny world of women and men with zip, with fresh spirit and new insights, who knows? You just may be outrageously successful.